Autobiography 1988

Hodee Waldstein Edwards

1914 - 2012

ISBN Print 979-8-9887747-6-1
ISBN eBook 979-8-9887747-5-4
Library of Congress Control Number: 2024921394

Published by Estuary Press
472 Skyline Drive,
Vallejo, California 94591

Autobiography 1988 consists of two essays by Hodee Edwards originally appearing in the "Frank Family Reunion Book," August, 1987, in Burlington, Vermont, edited by Joseph and Cathy Frank, and Beryl and Gloria Frank. Hodee's two essays, entitled "Hodee Waldstein Edwards," and "Bessie Waldstein Frank," published here by Estuary Press, are companion pieces to her book "Labor Aristocracy" (Estuary Press, 2024). Special thanks to Eva Lou Edwards for proofing and helping in many ways. I take responsibility for all errors that may have found their way into the text.

Contents

List of Images

Autobiography 1988

Hodee Waldstein Edwards

Born December 18, 1914
Parents: Bessie & Samuel Waldstein
Husband: Harvey Richards (d)
George Edwards (d)
Children: Steffen 1942, Paul 1944, Eva Lou 1950

I am Hodee Waldstein Edwards, first-born of Bessie Frank Waldstein and Samuel Harry Waldstein.

In real life, I am approaching my 73rd birthday. In the harsh world of jobs and employment, I can doctor a few facts and pass for 55 at the moment. I am fairly well pleased with my Self and my off-beat life.

JOSEPH AND DORA FRANK and their children, 1908. (left to right) 1st row Rachel, Max; 2nd row Sam, Dora, Joseph, Barnet; 3rd row Bessie, Mike, Jacob, Ben, Mary, Abe.

1. Mother: Bessie Frank Waldstein

Born: August 6, 1889
Parents: Dora & Joseph Frank Died: July 2, 1968,
Husband: Samuel Waldstein
Children: Hodee 1914, Hannah 1917, Alice 1919,
Mathew 1923

My grandmother, Dora Shufro Frank, had eleven children of whom ten grew up. My mother, Bessie Frank Waldstein, was the third child, and the first of three girls. Her birth date was August 6, 1889. She lived to be 79 and had four children, of whom I am the eldest, while our one brother, Mathew, died at 32 of multiple sclerosis, was the youngest.

Bessie Frank Waldstein

It is intensely interesting to me, trying at this distance to evaluate her life, to have to note that, of the four children she bore, two hated her - Alice and Mathew. Even one of my sons, who may have met her once, told me he hated her "for what she did to you, Mom." I am only now, in my old age, becoming aware of what that was.

The stories my mother told me about her childhood pictured her to me as a household drudge. Oldest girl in the family, my mother was expected to, and did, most of the housework in that big house in Burlington, Vermont. My grandmother did the cooking and baking, but due to her obesity, she was unable to climb stairs (in fact, her size even affected me: I never got to sit on Bobey's lap - there wasn't any.)

Dora Shufro Frank 1923

When she finished high school, my mother went to her father and said she wanted to go to college. His reply, without rancor, was, "For what should I educate a woman?" However, she kept bugging him until, finally, he said, "All right. Stay at home for one year. If, at the end of that time, you still must go to college, I promise I will send you." And to Joseph Elihu Frank, his word was his bond.

Sam and Bessie Waldstein

Knowing that, Bessie did her additional year of domestic servitude. On the exact anniversary of the promise, she appeared before her father and reminded him of their bargain.

This was how, in 1912, Bessie Frank became the first Jewish woman to graduate from the University of Vermont. She achieved a Bachelor's degree in ancient languages with both Phi Beta Kappa and cum laude. Not bad for a child who, though born in Burlington, Vermont, started school without being able to speak a word of English!

My mother never stopped studying and learning throughout her life. She was forever attending lectures or taking extension courses at nearby Harvard University. For example, she studied architecture and thereafter could look at any house and tell you correctly how the rooms inside were arranged. Out of the education she bought with that year of her life, my mother became, in my mind at least, undoubtedly the most erudite person I ever knew (and scholars - mostly male - passed by the truckload through our living room.) She did not flaunt her learning: she never ventured an unsolicited opinion. But if you had a question, about no matter what, she always came up a detailed, informative and interesting answer.

Her erudition, based on her formal and later self-education, probably contributed to her eye for fine Things. The capital letter is deliberate, for Things took first place in our life in the big house in Brookline, Massachusetts, where we grew up (I, after age four).

With this eye – and my father's money when he had it (my dad told me once that he was a millionaire on "three separate occasions in his life") my mother collected wonderful objects: Persian rugs, delicate china knick knacks, jewelry, bronzes, ceramics – all, of course, out of bounds to us children. Nonetheless, at least partly because of them, we lived in an aura of beauty.

Moreover, under her inspiring example, my father began to study. He taught himself to "recognize the New Masters," those painters of the day whose works we were able to buy because they, most of whose pictures now hang in the New York Metropolitan Museum of Art, were then literally starving in garrets as any artist worthy of his salt is suppose to do. So, besides all the beautiful Things, we also were raised amidst paintings by Max Weber, Bernard Karfiol, Natalie Goncharova, Kuniyoshi, and other well-knowns from the world of painting.

Hodee Waldstein, 1927

We also went on endless trips to local and nearby museums which, in themselves, were boring; but I loved their revelations of the ancient glories of other cultures, like that of Egypt.

I loved equally those seven years during which my mother, my dad, my next younger sister Hannah, and I went to the Saturday night concerts of the Boston Symphony Orchestra. Our seats were in the first balcony, left, directly over the mighty organ, so that we were in full view of its conductor of the time, Serge Koussevitzky. "Kouss" always acknowledged our presence - two small girls with sausage curls and dark velvet dresses with wide lace collars - by bowing gravely to us. We always graciously returned his bows.

My mother had another side to her that she hid from most of her friends. Today, it is called ESP, extra-sensory perception. She had a certain instinct for people which rarely if ever went awry. My father told me of a time when he introduced a prospective business associate to my mother. She was a stickler for manners. Yet, in this instance, when the gentleman thrust forward his hand to acknowledge the introduction, Bessie's hand went impulsively to her back. When my father later chided her, she told him the man was no good and intended him no good. Naturally, my father, a good, solid, non-superstitious citizen, ignored her warning. But sure enough, he later confessed, not long afterwards the man mounted a deliberate campaign aimed at destroying my father's business.

Furthermore, whenever we went places by street car, my mother always took seats right behind the motorman's closed-in cab at the very front of the car. I would have preferred not to have to stare at the polished bare brown wood, but to sit closer to the door facing other people so I could watch them and what they did. When finally I got up courage to ask my mother why she did this, her explanation was, "If I sit where I can see people's faces, it's like noise. Very disturbing. I can hear them thinking."

Despite this, despite all her intellectual prowess, despite objects d'art, the paintings, the Things, my mother was frozen inside. For one bit of evidence, she was afraid of dogs. We could be walking calmly along a street together; then, let some miserable pooch appear and she'd suck in her breath and whisper, "Go away! Go away! Go home!" I experienced her panic and for years was also afraid of dogs. We had cats at home, but that was because we shared the house with mice. It was the servants who cared for them.

My mother was not a candid person, especially not with her children, who were told just as much or as little as she decided we needed or were entitled to hear, which wasn't much, either on the surrounding facts of our life together as a family or on the emotional side. So it must have been heavy on her mind when one day she told me that, on the day her pre-college year of housework was up, she resolved that she would never again in life do housework.

From the start, our mother raised us all according to a book written by a man who was the "Dr. Spock" of the era: "The Care and Feeding of the Child," by Lewis   Emmett Holt. Dr. Holt was responsible for the emotional destruction of a whole generation of children; at least, those in the middle class. I was one. What the august Dr. Holt said was that you never, never pick a child up when it cries; never give in on discipline, but insist on rigidly maintaining it. Otherwise, he opined, your child would grow up with "complexes." (For an interesting discussion of the impact of Dr. Holt on the American family, read "Touch – The Human Significance of the Skin," by Ashley Montagu.)

For example, when I was put to bed at night - this was before I was five, but I remember the scenes vividly and uncomfortably - the dark green window shades were pulled down and out went my mother, firmly closing the door behind her. I could not overcome my sense of loss, of sinking, of being abandoned by that closing door. I would plead, as it closed, "Mama, please leave the door open just a teensy bit."

She never said she wouldn't; she just didn't. At which point, I would set up and wail: "I wann-na drink of wad-der." I would howl it once and wait. Naturally, no reply. So, I would try again. After the third attempt, I would set up a continuing sing-song until our upstairs neighbors would start banging on the steam pipes.

So, in effect, it was thanks to Dr. Lewis Emmett Holt that we had to move out of that apartment on Parkman Street. Dr. Holt's advice was followed, I now believe, because it totally exonerated my mother from having to give us what she did not have to give. Dr. Holt not only condoned her acquired coldness but, a well-known "authority", he represented her unfortunate condition as absolutely the "best thing" for her children.

The place my dad bought, 123 Babcock Street in Brookline, had eight bedrooms, a full basement (hardly utilized) and three stories. It had been built in his heyday by a successful lumber

123 Babcock Street, Brookline, MA

merchant named Mr. Blanchard. It surely was big enough for me to holler my head off in, but the necessity never again arose: my bedroom was on the third floor. After we moved there, my mother began dealing her emotional problems via a heart condition (a leaking valve) and migraine headaches. These complaints gave her, among other benefits, a reason not to be able to visit the third floor very often. I'm sure the complaints were real; I'm not sure that they had to develop, had proper help been available.

I am not sure, either, what the cause was for her total inability to love - or, at least, to express it. I only remember seeing my parents fight once. I cannot recall what it was about, except that it was very scary to me. My dad used to kiss mama's cheek a lot in our presence, but no other affectionate gestures that I can recall ever passed between them for me to see, nor do I recollect mama ever returning any of those kisses on the cheek. Furthermore, not once in my whole life from earliest childhood do I recall her ever hugging or otherwise affectionately touching us, her children. We were expected to plant a good-night or hello kiss on her cool cheek, but I do not remember its ever being returned.

My parents were quite frank in letting us know why there were three of us female children: no male had as yet been produced. When I was eight years old, one finally did appear. He proved a huge disappointment to his parents: he was no flaming intellectual; but a simple, probably dyslexic, guy good with his hands mechanically, but was never allowed or aided to develop such skills because they were regarded as "common" or "vulgar". Late in his 20's my brother was diagnosed as having multiple sclerosis; the military service assumed responsibility for it till they could no longer do anything for his condition (he served in the U.S. Coast Guard during World War II).

Mathew Waldstein,
c. 1946

One of my sister's, Alice, told me with some heat that she "hated our mother" and she referred to Anna Maxwell as responsible for any happiness she may have had in life. Anna Maxwell was a Canadian woman who worked in a domestic capacity for my mother. She "lived in," her room being on the same third floor with mine and that of Alice.

Well, Anna had the misfortune to fall in love with a man named Harry. Harry was a "good Jewish man." Although she bore him two sons, he would never marry her because "she was a shiksah." This was during an era when having so-called illegitimate children could get one booted out of a job. But not Anna. My mother made it possible for Anna to place her sons in Canada on her sister's ranch, where she could visit them during her vacations.

During the Great Depression which began in November of 1929, a whole year went by when my father had zero income. My mother fed us all on credit (of which she later repaid every cent) from S.S. Pierce Company, a posh grocery store at Coolidge Corner. Right away, she told Anna Maxwell, "Anna, as things are, I can no longer pay you. So if you want to seek other employment, I'll do what I can to help you find it." Anna's reply was, "If I have to work for you forever for nothing, Mrs. Waldstein, I'll be happy to."

She stayed (and here, too, my mother eventually paid her all her back wages). We children were, I should mention, never taken into our parents' confidence in this, as in other matters. As a result, my mother received a new nickname. She had earlier been known as "Teaball" due to the quantities of tea she drank. But, as "seconds" became unavailable at mealtimes during this no-income year, she became "Old Lady Pinchpenny."

Anna Maxwell's story was not an isolated incident in my mother's dealings with people (outside the family of course). I cite it because to me it illuminates my mother's natural inclinations as good and kind ones. Everywhere possible, she helped various people, dispensing kindnesses. She was highly praised and esteemed by her friends and acquaintances.

Once, toward the end of her life, my mother accused herself to one of my sisters (who reported it to me) of not being "a Good Mother." For me, this sad, self-accusing remark came as a beautiful flash of insight. From the point of view of white middle class U.S. Jewish society as it was in her lifetime, it was true. Not only was she not a stereotyped "Good Mother;" she was conscious of her "failure" to live up to her society's expectations for women.

So, Bessie Frank Waldstein's "failure" as a mother was not embodied solely in her inability to love or express love. That was only a particular single expression of her non-conformity and may or may not have been a result of her individual reaction to some possible unknown childhood trauma.

In those days, the only "aid" for such problems came from Sigmund Freud, whom I prefer to remember as Sigmund Fraud. She didn't need to be told she was suffering from penis-envy, thank you. She needed help that, today, is only just gradually becoming available. My mother's dislike of sex, her inability to show – or perhaps even to feel - love today are becoming recognized as symptoms of inner-family relationships in childhood that were flawed just as often by non-sexual factors as by sex.

But by itself, this problem need not have made her a misfit who couldn't conform to the society in which she found herself. What did that was her too keen mind; her too all-seeing eyes. She thought incisively ("like a man"?). How uppity of her! Nor was she willfully frozen in her inner-family life; it was because she couldn't help it.

At the same time, I wish I could have heard her say that she wasn't a "Good Mother: I'd have told her that I honor her for that so-called failure. For, seeing the past with today's eyes, I know now that she was a remarkable, unique soul, buried before death under the debris of centuries of Jewish, White or of any male-dominated society's self-defensive hatred of women.

In any case, I do not hate her. The son of mine who says he does claims that my remark, "I feel sorry for her," is humiliating to her and condescending. Be that as it may, for now, that is the feeling I have for her. With her great rich wealth of knowledge and her natural instinct for helping others, she should have had a joyous and fulfilling life. I don't think she did.

That she did not, despite her life in dad's "white elephant," as she always called our residence, was to me clearly evidenced by what happened to her after our father died in 1941. She "never got over it," as the saying goes. She went back to the synagogue, which she left when I was about five because my father had become a militant atheist and forbade us to enroll in any church until we reached majority (at which time what we did was to devolve upon our own heads). She took up painting and the few examples I have seen suggest an inner power of which none of us were ever made aware in any positive way during our sojourn at her side in childhood. For years she flitted around and dithered and finally wound up in a nursing home. Any money she got hold of, she frantically and promptly gave away, until my father's executor, his youngest brother, Uncle Ben, took it all away from her and established a trust fund with enough for her to live on but not enough to throw away.

Through all this, I'm sure her constant comparison of her own role in her family that of some of her friends must have been a heavy factor exaggerating her feelings of guilt and lack of self worth.

No matter what anyone says, despite her obviously crippled emotional development from whatever childhood disaster which prevented her from ever realizing her full great potential, I believe that Bessie Frank did contribute four good human beings to this earth. She was - and insisted that we all be - rigidly honest. She made me whatever I am today. She was the one who told me that I was never to fear stating my honestly held opinions no matter what anyone else said or did. I lived that way and paid dearly for it, but my life is thereby the richer, even if not in money. However, she would always add, if ever anyone can prove to you logically that you are wrong, you must never be so inflexible as not to admit your error and change. I have tried to carry that out, too. I have found that it leads to a wonderful independence of soul which makes life intense and lastingly attractive.

So let her rest in peace: Bessie Frank Waldstein, a modest, unassuming giant of an intellect, a grievously injured soul. In her family life, she may not have measured up to "Marmy" in "Little Women" and her children all paid for her unresolved, probably unrecognized, emotional problems. But overall, in life, she was truly "a real mensch." She would have liked hearing that, too.

2. Childhood

I was born at 7 a.m. on a cold winter's day in Allston, Massachusetts (now a suburb of Boston), on December 18, in 1914, which also happened to be the eighth light of Channukah in that year. For years, my birthday was celebrated on that eighth light, regardless of calendar date.

The family into which I was born belonged to the well-to-do liberal/progressive Jewish intellectual world of Boston, with its emphasis on culture, honesty and freedom of self-expression. It was during World War I, already under way in Europe "to make the world safe for democracy. "

I was born at home, which was an apartment on Brighton Street off Harvard Avenue. Although we must have moved from there before I was three years old, I have a few memories of Allston: the

Infant Hodee on Mother's lap. Sam to her right. 1915

delicatessen right across Harvard Avenue where the old, white-mustachioed proprietor, who stood always with bent knees, made little chuckling noises when we talked, fit each visit, he would hand me incredibly delicious kosher pickles and brown pretzels with crunchy crystallized salt baked onto them.

I also have dim recollections of a huge double bed with my mother lying in it, propped up on pillows, wearing pince-nez glasses that wiggled when she moved, shooting small light darts all over the room, creating a display so fascinating that I couldn't pay attention to what she was saying.

I had evidently been born in that very bed, a ten-pound child, which had led the hopeful parents to believe that their first child would be a boy. Alas! Only a girl! My childhood, and indeed my life, were molded by the huge disappointment that my entrance into the family in female form caused my Jewish father. However intellectual he may have become over the years, his anti-female bias prevailed against me from the moment I appeared.

Not long before my third birthday, we moved to a ground-floor apartment in Parkman Street, Brookline, where we stayed till I was almost five. This was a peaceful middle class Jewish neighborhood with a row of apartment houses facing each other down the street and a field at one end. Horse-drawn wagons crunched and creaked along it on weekdays, bearing great blue ice blocks for the clumsy iceboxes of the time. The other kids got to suck juicily on ice chips left behind when the Ice Man cut the big blocks for customers. Not Hodee! The ice might be dirty!

In that apartment, on occasion, it was impressed upon me how worthless a girl-child is.

Take a bleak fall morning, for example. My sister Hannah, about a year old, is in my Dad's arms. My mother, as usual, is propped up in the big bed. The huge window looks out on a large cement yard enclosed on all sides by the backs of apartment houses.

Against one such apartment house stands a row of garbage cans, lids tilted at crazy angles in expectation of Garbage Men who will soon empty them into great trucks. My father is talking - ostensibly to Hannah.

"You see those garbage cans out there," he is asking my sister. My nose resting on the window sill, I feel my eyes glued to them.

"Well," he continues, "that's where your Mother and I wanted to throw both of you, because you were girls."

A gray prickly silence enfolds me, piercing my eye-balls. I picture myself under one of those tilted can covers, A great hullabaloo arises: the Garbage Men are here! I feel myself hoisted roughly, suddenly, skyward as the can is tipped sharply over till I spill, with the rest of the garbage, into the smelly inside of the truck, in a moment, it will grind the entire mess up into pig food.

In this Parkman Street apartment there was always a live-in maid to do the cooking and housework. There was also a nurse-maid. Marion Yarofsky, the woman who started by taking care of just me; and then, after Hannah's birth, of her as well, adored and made much of me.

Hannah, a chubby little ball of babyhood with flaming red hair and dumpling cheeks, did not clamor for as much attention as I did and, accordingly, got less. My mother noticed that Hannah was being more or less ignored — and that was the end of Marion Yarofsky. Or, maybe I'd become too attached to her, too.

Another result of his disappointment in me was that my Dad, who had arrived in this country at age four, shrewd, brilliant, and energetic with high hopes for a future envisioned in sons, created a myth around my person. This myth declaimed that I (had to be) was his little "Leonardo da Vance," as he always dubbed that great historic figure. Incidents like the above impressed upon me my need, on pain of virtual extinction, to live up to my father's Role Model for me. If I couldn't do right and be a Boy, the least I could do to justify my existence was to be or become Super-Girl. For years I strove mightily to live up to this expectation.

At first, I had aimed to become a boy. I developed a swaggering walk, talked in as low a voice as possible; practiced throwing balls the way boys do; kicked footballs . . . I got pretty good at all of it – but it soon became apparent that I would not become a Boy no matter what.

So then, my goal (unstated to myself, but motivating my every action) became to surpass all known males in excellence - and for our family, that meant, quite simply, in scholarship. In this, for years, I succeeded. I wrote poetry, painted, sculpted, played violin and won almost all prizes at school. It took 50 years for me to recognize the myth in its entirety, its effect on my life, to reject it and cast about for something else to build and live by and with.

But in those days, with his myth almost palpably enveloping us, my father would talk to me as if I had been a son.

"Never be a Joiner," he would admonish, over and over. "You have to write a book that will show others The Way." This oft-repeated thought was not really clear to me. What book? Why? WHY should I want to be "better" than "others" (whoever they might be) and make them follow me? To where?

Yet, because of these talks, which were about his ambitions, his views on life, politics, culture and whatever was the Topic of the Day, I learned to think as males do: aggressively, argumentatively, incisively. That did not win me points later, in the female world. But, by the time I understood that, it was too late to do anything about it (luckily for me, I now feel).

As to my mother's influence (some of which will be found in Chapter 1 in this volume), she taught me to read; she taught me obedience, and she gave me standards and values. She also had a unique method of punishment: never spankings; it was "taking away privileges," and she wasn't kidding about that. From her, there was no praise; good behavior and top scholastic achievement were simply expected – and therefore, by and large, they happened.

But my mother, with the best of intentions, also did one thing to me that blighted a couple of areas of my life. I was born left-handed. However, following the custom of the time, with her stern unyielding will, she forced me to change to right-handed. The result, about which I learned the meaning only very recently, was twofold: I lost my sense of direction; and a certain flaw developed in my sense of rhythm such that I never could learn to do ballroom dancing, an activity I would give my (still extant) eye teeth to be able to do.

The world we lived in was strictly a White world. There may have been black people around, but you rarely saw them. A vivid incident sticks with me involving one of those rare glimpses.

There was a girl named Jean who lived on our street. Jean had a brother (lucky child!) and Brother had a bike. One day, Jean's mother sent her to the janitor's apartment to see if the janitor had seen or put away Brother's apparently missing bike. Jean asked me to go with her. She said she was afraid to go to the apartment alone.

Blithely, I agreed.

Out a back door, onto the big rear cement center of the apartment complex and across it, we went, and into the back of another building. There, we began to descend some steep, winding wooden steps into a sub-basement. Ahead of me, Jean knocked at a door facing the bottom step. Sound of footsteps. The door opened.

A tall woman in a cotton dress with a small child clinging to her skirt stood in the doorway. She and the child had velvety black skin, the first I ever remember seeing. Looking upward at her dignified face, I glimpsed the unusually long pillar of her neck. Jean opened her mouth. Instead of inquiring about the bike, as I expected, she let out an unearthly shriek, turned and stumbled back up the stairs. Having not the foggiest notion of what had occasioned the scream, I nonetheless caught its panic. So I too screeched and bolted up the wedge-shaped steps.

In the years that followed, I remembered that stately woman, her long neck and clinging child many times, each with a shrinking inside. Why? Why had I screamed at her ordinary presence? That was my introduction to the Black World where I was later to live for over two decades.

My main distinction on Parkman Street was that my mother did not "believe in" dolls. But one fine day, permission was granted to visit the nearby apartment of Elsie Wyzanski, who may have been six or seven. Elsie had a "Mama" doll as big as I was. She stood propped up by a metal frame. If you tipped her backward, her eyes closed; if you tipped her forward, she bleated, "Maaa...ma." I remember the doll in detail; of Elsie, only her name and an impression of dark hair remain.

Probably the most significant event of our Parkman Street years for me physically was that I spent a year in bed with a fever. The doctors claimed not to know its cause, so kept me in bed. I never felt sick. I did my prescribed "resting" in my Dr. Denton PJ's with their built-in feet by jumping up and down on my knees on the springy hard mattress whenever Mama was absent.

One day during the course of this illness, my Dad came home early from work. I remember him, sailing into my bedroom in his overcoat and fedora hat. He told me to get out of bed and get dressed. "Why?" I asked. "Where are we going?" My father smiled and replied, "Where the stars bloom and roses shine."

This was typical: Nothing, however much it affected me, was ever explained or discussed with me in advance.

Our destination turned out to be Children's Hospital on Longwood Avenue in Brookline. I stayed there a while for the doctors to explore the nature of my fever. My mother had a cot in the hospital room and stayed with me. However, never at any time does my memory show her to me intervening to save me from the horrors that there befell me.

I was no longer a baby in my own eyes; yet the hospital personnel dumped me into a crib. Furthermore, they had the guts to pull up the sides, as if I were totally incompetent. There I saw my first Japanese person in the form of an intern in a white coat who drooped by, sat on the edge of my bed, said nary a word, but thumped the cold flat circular end of his stethoscope onto cry unceremoniously bared skinny flat bony chest. Later, my mother explained that there were millions of people who looked like that; they were not different from others; they just looked different. Oh.

I can recall nothing that happened to me there which was not an indignity. For instance, a nurse or two would appear, and without a word, would peel off my hospital pajamas and wrap me in an army blanket so both arms were pinned immovably to my sides. I was whisked in and out of elevators, most of them descending, and finally stuffed between two long dark glass plates. Someone said that pictures were being taken of my insides. I had never seen a camera like that, so I didn't believe it, firmly expecting to die some horrible death.

The whole stay was characterized by similar terrors arid a knowledge of being complete helpless. Everything was done to me, not for me. Oh, Dr. Holt! For your endorsement of the "children must be seen and not heard" dictum, I do hate you all the way from here to eternity!

I think it was not long after that that my mother got me out of bed "to try to live a normal life", against doctors' advice. In my case, "normality" included never being permitted to take gym class with the other kids in school; having to take naps long past any respectable nap-taking age for children (I never went to sleep, so those were boring, endless times); and each day, having my temperature taken at least twice, in public if need be. Because of the fever and that year spent in bed, I also missed going to kindergarten except for two days which I remember vividly, including the teacher's name - "Miss Bean," a moniker I found excruciatingly funny.

The whole hospital episode, of such duration and filled with such negative emotions, and its aftermath together form a logical enough explanation for the years I have spent, and continue to spend, in the U.S. "Health Movement." I enjoy good health now, and nobody takes my temperature any more without my consent.

That year in bed and its accompanying treatment also helped to form my existing contempt for the "Medical (so-called) Profession" in this land, though I know in my head that there must be some "good individuals" among them. My own personal experience with the breed is not the only factor reinforcing my current attitude toward them. But that experience did offer a seed bed for its fertile development.

By and large, since the early 1970's, I stay away from doctors. Except in moments of temporary panic or weakness, I refuse to take "their" drugs. I eat as much "Health Food" and organic produce as I can lay hands on. In short, I am an on-going Health Nut who enjoys every minute of it.

Just before I was five, due to Dr. Lewis Emmett Holt and his influence on my mother, (for this information, see Chapter 1: Mother, in this volume) we moved away from Parkman Street into a large, three-story white house, sitting on half an acre of lawn at the end of a block on Babcock Street in a Brookline area where no Jews had lived before.

My father was able to buy the place because the local realtors were trying to force the widow who wanted to sell it to lower her price. My Dad just knocked on the door, accepted her quote of $75,000, and asked if he could step inside and write her a check, so he told me.

We might have settled in without too much hullabaloo had it not been for my mother's obsession against "Boys." We were early instructed that "Boys are Bad" (despite the contradictory fact that my being born a girl was an implied cardinal sin). You did not play with boys; certainly, you did not allow them into your spacious yard to play.

"We bought this yard for you children to play in," I remember my mother intoning to me on more than one occasion, always adding, "and you will play in it and nowhere else."

The neighborhood nestled almost at the feet and in the shadow of nearby St. Aiden's Church. All our neighbors were Catholics. As far as we (my sisters and I) and those children are concerned, I recall no friction. Instead, as soon as Mama went off on some errand, we called the neighbor kids in. Most, but not all, were boys, though at least one had a sister who came along. He had a lot of fun in that big yard. There were so many places to hide.

But we'd get to playing so hard, we'd forget to keep our eye out for Mama's return. First thing we'd know, there'd be a sharp loud hostile clicking from an upstairs window: Mama was rapping her wedding ring on the glass. She'd open the window and holler at the kids to get out. Her words reached only receding backs as the visitors scattered through the back gate onto Stetson Street, where most of them lived.

That happened several times. Obviously, each incident was duly reported to parents whose comments one can imagine from the result. For, one day, we three girls came out in our back yard to play as usual and within seconds, all the kids we knew were running around our yard, yelling, "Dirty Jews! Dirty Jews! Dirty Jews! Yaaaahh!" And they were throwing stones at us.

Not one to take stone-throwing, especially at me, lightly, I determined that if these kids wanted a fight, I'd give them a good one. I corralled my two sisters, telling them to gather up stones. I set up a bastion at our mulberry tree, whose branches hung around its trunk in a green oval to the ground, creating a perfect place to become invisible from outside the barberry hedge that bounded our property. I think my sisters, seeing my grim, dirt-smudged face, early on high-tailed it for the back porch and safety. I was too busy to notice: hostile stones flew at me; mine, at them. Then, I made what I considered a "lucky" connection: I hit Joe Cummings in the temple and down he went in a pool of blood.

Well, that earned me plenty of momentary attention. My Dad was summoned home early from work. It must have been at least June, because the sun porch screen enclosure was up. He took me out there and set me on his knee (in itself an unprecedented event) to try to persuade me of the error of my ways. His bird-like hazel eyes were blinking rapidly as he informed me, "That's not how we deal with our enemies." A peculiar smile twisted his bluish lips.

Pretty soon, the cop on the beat, old Mr. Keliher with his iron-grey walrus mustache, clumped up the front porch steps in his huge black cop shoes with their round-domed toes. He took me by the hand and led me to the side of the road.

"Look at that puddle of blood," he exhorted. "Just see what you have done!" He didn't say it accusingly; rather, sorrowfully.

I squatted down there on the edge of Steadman Street and gazed into the dark sticky pool in the soft tar. I could see white fluffy clouds scudding over its surface. "I hope he dies," I kept muttering between clenched teeth. "I hope he dies." And I stuck to that refrain; nothing my father said to me budged me.

The irony of the whole incident is that my fury vented itself for the "wrong" reason. Being called a Jew was no biggie for me; it wasn't news. I KNEW and accepted that I was a Jew and that nothing on God's Green Earth could or would change that fact, just as it could not change my being a girl. But most decidedly, it was nothing short of base slander to term "dirty" a girl who regularly, every single Saturday night, took her weekly bath.

Probably the summer I was eight, I was sent to camp at a place on Lake Gregmere near Peterborough in New Hampshire. From that summer, I recall "Aunt Psyche," one of the counselors, who insisted that I could, too, write a poem for the camp newspaper.

"Here's a piece of paper," she said. "Write about a bird."

I wrote:

"Up in a tree one day
"Sat a bluebird on a branch that sweetly swayed.
"He sang, 'Too-whit, too-who,'
"and then he flew away."

It was published. Such a beginning! Yet, ever since, whenever anyone has asked what I "did," I always said I was "a writer."

3. School Girl

From the age of five, I took piano lessons with a lady friend of my mother's named Sophie Goldman. Her husband, Hiram, taught violin; her two sons were David and Danny. When at eight years of age, I balked at further piano practicing, I was turned over to Hiram. Two years later, my mother took me to M. Georges Fourel, a very tall man with bent knees, round rosy cheeks and white hair, who played viola in the Boston Symphony Orchestra.

This lucky occurrence came out of our Boston Symphony Orchestra concert-going. (See Chapter 1: Mother) It probably also resulted from certain "Soirees" which our parents held at our home for the elite of Jewish intellectual Boston and vicinity. A number of men from the Boston Symphony attended these and undoubtedly one of them must have recommended M. Fourel.

When I started with him, M. Fourel told my Mother that Hiram had ruined me and that he would have to spend the first months or years making me unlearn all I had been taught. For nine years, I took lessons from M. Fourel, adoring him and trying my best. Once he learned that I was studying French in school, he never again spoke to me in English. At the same time, as I lacked syntax and vocabulary, I always replied to him in English.

He also told my mother I "had talent." But the truth was that I could hear every sour note I manufactured on those strings and knew I'd never be the great violinist that, as with anything else I attempted, my parents expected of me. So, at 17, I quit taking violin lessons.

I finally donated the expensive violin my mother had bought for me to the fancy school my sons were attending in Verde Valley, near Sedona, in Arizona, some time in the 1950s.

I can't remember what age I was when my Dad first started studying aesthetics. I do remember that a succession of paintings made their way across our walls and down into the basement. And accompanying this material procession there was also a more human one: for whenever there was money, Dad liked to entertain these "rising" artists to dinner at our home. So there was Mr. Raskin, whom (of course) we all called Rat-skin; there was Mr. Manievich, who walked pigeon-toed and had a smooth black page-boy bob and two beautiful daughters, Lucy and Manya, one as blond as the other was brunette. He and the daughters got the most invitations. And finally, I recall Howard Gibbs, whom my mother declared was "an Adonis," but whose mouth tilted too much to an angle for me to agree to that. He managed to bilk my Dad out of two years in Paris in return "for the pick of his paintings on return." My Dad's pick showed he was educating his eye: it turned out to be a forgery taken from an Andre Derain.

When I was eleven, my Dad, who was still studying Art and learning to "educate his eye," brought me home a supply of oil paints, brushes arid pochards (canvas stretched onto stiff cardboard and ready to work on). My first work was a still life, showing a shapely white pitcher and some fruit and it didn't look at all bad for a first attempt. I kept at it.

My parents took me to Abrahama Levinson, an artist headquartered in Rockport, Massachusetts, "to learn about painting." We went to him, first because they and the Levinsons had become friends; and second because my Dad had decided that Levinson was a "good colorist." The teacher was forbidden to give me lessons in the art of mixing colors, or any other technique. He was merely to comment on finished paintings I had done, from which comments, I was supposed to learn. This was because my Dad firmly believed that "Art teachers destroy more artists than any other single cause, including poverty."

At one point, Robert Vose of the famous Vose Gallery wanted to give an exhibition of my paintings. But my mother turned it down. She said that he only wanted to show the paintings because they were done by a 17-year-old; not because they were good. As usual, she was right.

I attended public school in Brookline. Grammar school was the Edward Devotion School, which sat on land that had a small wooden house on it at the front. This, we learned, was a historic home in which had lived the man named Edward Devotion, a local Hero of the American Revolutionary War. I have vague memories about the school insofar as my performance is concerned.

When I had been registered in kindergarten for those two days, my Dad had taken me. He had registered me as "Helen Waldstein." He told my mother he could not bring himself to saddle me with a handle like "Hodee." He also registered me under the same name in First Grade. As a result, when Second Grade began, my mother took me to school. Said Mama, "This child has a name and she is going to use it."

The teacher was Miss Abbott. All I remember of second grade is the dread moment when Miss Abbott called upon me to recite. "HOD-ee," she blared, pronouncing the first syllable like the receptacle in which we carried coal upstairs for the kitchen stove, the hod. With sinking heart and burning cheeks, I slowly stood up amidst a flurry of whispering and giggling. I didn't enjoy the first few days, but I'm glad my mother did that. I like having my own, "unusual", name.

In 7th grade, I was in Miss Malloy's class. Miss Malloy taught us English grammar. I enjoyed every minute of that instruction and am eternally grateful to that elderly woman, with her pouter pigeon shape, double chins, big brown freckles and hair piled in a doughnut atop her head, for teaching me the structure of the language I use.

In that grade, too, I joined the other girls of my age in having a "crush" on one of the teachers. All the others chose bonnie Miss Fitzhenry, with her blue eyes, dark eyelashes and hair and her angelic countenance. Not I! No, I settled on the geography teacher,

Miss Florence Lewis. She was a tall, rather masculine looking woman with short-cut blond hair and rimless spectacles. She had a well-earned reputation for being tough. Even the worst boys behaved in her classes.

Just because everyone else said how horrible she was, I conceived an adoration for Miss Lewis. I painted small still lives (one, I recall, was a potato) and presented them to her. I stayed after school just to be allowed to erase her blackboard. And I scared the livin' bejeepers out of her. So one day she took me out onto the balcony of the school auditorium.

She said she hoped that when I thought of her in later years, it would be with kindly thoughts. Indeed, with no other! Moreover, now that I think of it, her sternness, her insistence on and success in maintaining discipline was reminiscent of my mother. Maybe I needed to have my "Mother" love me even if I had to "buy" that with gifts of paintings and whatnot from a surrogate.

Probably far more significant in my life than any of the honors I took or friends I made was an incident in which I became involved in High School, the outcome of which colored my entire future.

A number of the people in my class were assigned to a Special English Class for their ability to express themselves. The teacher of this class in our Junior Year was one Miss Spaulding. This tall gray-haired lady with her pointed face and mouth slightly askew was very proud of her "pure" American (I guess, meaning British) ancestry. She had a red-haired English setter who came to school with her and sat silently and patiently at her feet as she taught us our special English. She also amused our infantile minds by constantly referring to "my son." She had an adopted boy at home. To our little minds, just coming into the Great Big World, having anyone named MISS Spaulding talk about her SON was just too too utterly utter.

One day the Lieutenant Governor of the State of Massachusetts was slated to be the speaker in our weekly or monthly Assembly.

For our homework assignment that evening, our patriotic teacher told us to learn all the verses of the "Star Spangled Banner." On the way home from school, my indignation against this infantile assignment grew. By the time my girl friend Miriam and I had reached my home (hers was a few hundred feet further along across Steadman Street), I announced, "Heck! That sure is a dumb assignment for a special English class. I am not going to do it." "Me, either," agreed Mimsie, nobly and loyally.

Next day, when we arrived in English class, what does Miss Spaulding do but put paper in front of each of us. I knew I was trapped. Never one to run from, but rather to meet, Trouble, I stood up at my front row desk and, quaking like a drowning rat, declared, "Miss Spaulding, I did not do the assignment."

She came and loomed over me, looking down her long straight nose at me through rimless spectacles that jiggled."Indeed!" she intoned, "And why NOT, may I ask?"

A terrible hush settled down onto the class. Amidst it, I heard the sound of my own voice saying, "I am opposed to nationalistic measures." A shocked pause from Teacher. Then she let me know publicly that my beliefs had nothing to do with obeying her instructions about which homework to do.

At this point, Mimsie decided she might as well throw in the towel, too. She said, "I didn't do it either,

Miss Spaulding."

"And your reason?" asked our instructor, coldly.

I held my breath. I think the whole class did, too.

Then, "Same reason," I heard Mimsie whisper. (I still love her.)

It turned out that ten of us had had the same reaction to the assignment as I, and had neglected to do it. All loyally insisted that they, too, "were opposed to nationalistic measures." Whether any of us knew its exact meaning, 1 am not sure. In any case, we were all kept after school, forced to write what we did remember of the anthem, graded accordingly (mine was a mind-blowing "D" because I found I didn't really know the words of even the first verse to the national anthem).

Before we were released to go home, we were lectured by the New England paragon. She told us that to her it was "very interesting" that eight of the ten of us who had refused this patriotic assignment were the "children of immigrants." There wasn't a one of us, including the two non-Jews, who didn't understand this delicate anti-Semitic remark for what it was.

A while later, my French teacher of the time, Katie O'Brien (with whom I remained friends to the recent end of her long life) asked me why I had done it. To her I told the truth, that the assignment was stupid. Katie said, "I know, Hodee. But this will follow you all the rest of your life." How right she was! I think she knew that because she spent every summer in France, so that her view of America was less provincial than that of natives who never leave these shores.

Despite this sensational incident, I did very well in High School. One honor I secured there, either in my Sophomore or my Junior year, was to win a behind-the-screen contest for the position of Concert Master in the High School Orchestra. I won it over Bernard Walkierie, whose father played second violin in the Boston Symphony Orchestra. Bernard could play faster than I, but I played in tune far oftener.

When I graduated from Brookline High in 1932, I took all the honors they gave except mathematics, including the American History prize, which I had snatched from the Seniors in my Junior Year with an essay written under a male pseudonym and enclosed in a faceless envelope which revealed the real name of the writer only after the prize was awarded.

Whence the phrase that I used to substitute for my reluctance to tell a teacher that I thought her homework assignment "stupid" came into my mouth, I did not then know, though I know now.

For I am sure this must have been one of the phrases which flew around in the smoke-blue air of those "Soirees" which my parents held in our home all the time I was growing up.

Among the fascinating people who attended one or more of these, I remember the Zighera brothers: the shorter one with the artistic mop of black hair played cello in the Boston Symphony; his tall thin pock-marked brother, Bernard, was the Symphony's harpist. I found especially endearing Boaz Pillar, a blue-jawed dimple-chinned broad Dutchman who played contra-bassoon there. He had married a beautiful woman (so it was said; I never saw her) who could not speak the same foreign language as he. Mama used to say, a bit breathlessly, that "how they managed to communicate is a big mystery, you know...ha ha ha."

There were others not from the Symphony. There was my father's friend "Ike" Goldberg, Professor of Spanish American Literature at Harvard and author of a biography of my idol, Havelock Ellis (with whom I corresponded for ten years, from age 15 to 25, all of which letters were later lost in Africa). He was also the music critic on the Boston Transcript. With him always came his chunky bob-haired wife, Elsie, who had a high screechy, tinkly laugh that could be heard above any noise in the conversation-filled room. She quietly saw to it that I got my share of the marvelous food for which I was supposed to wait till everyone else was served.

Another music critic was Stephen Somervell, with his wispy crown of blond curls and a chin dimple every bit as impressive as that of Boaz Pillar. He had a romantic limp, acquired in England following World War I, through all four years of which he had come unscathed only to be crippled for life in an ironic peace-time accident. Stephen could and did read music scores the way you and I read books.

He had a fabulous "mistress" named Beth Borton, a veritable Dresden doll in appearance, with her smooth heart-shaped face, her enormous pale blue eyes, and her smooth blondish hair, parted in the middle and worn in the old English fashion in a bun at the nape of her neck. She looked as if she should be wearing hoop skirts. She also worked for a living, though at what I doubt I ever heard, but it was considered daring at the time.

My "Uncle Abe," an official psychiatrist for the State of Massachusetts and one of those assigned to examine Nicolas Sacco of the famed Sacco and Vanzetti duo, author of a book entitled, "The Nervous Housewife," was usually present with his wife Dora.

But best of all were Nicholas Slonimsky, a musicologist later of world renown, then secretary to Serge Koussevitzky, and his wife Dorothy Adlow, art critic of the Christian Science MONITOR. At least once during each evening, Nicholas would respond to requests to play the piano (we had two: an upright Steinmetz in the hall and a black baby grand Bechstein in the "pink parlor.") Nicholas would play with an orange in each hand, or do "The Gollywog Cakewalk" standing with his back to the piano. Otherwise, he lay on the floor, reading our huge Funk & Wagnall dictionary as if it were a story book. From time to time, he would stop all conversations with a high-pitched command to "Leessen to theess! Leessen to theess!" And he would read off the definition of some obscure ten-syllable word, which forever after became a firm part of his vocabulary.

Dorothy, his wife, had a dark, mysterious beauty characterized by enchanting dimples, and she, too, had a romantic limp. She also had a charming sister named Chippe Adlow, who was married to a geologist named Bob whom I never recall meeting. The Christian Science MONITOR subsequently sent Dorothy to the young Soviet Union to critique its art. Dorothy returned from there with a burning enthusiasm, not so much for its art as for its cooperative child-care, for she and Nicholas had produced one daughter, Electra, the apple of their eye.

Her enthusiasm persuaded Nicholas to revisit the Soviet Union at his brother's long-time invitation. There, he conducted an orchestra before an audience of working people in jeans and babushkas, whose loudly expressed enthusiasm for what he was doing changed

Nicholas, refugee from the 1917 Revolution, into a pro-Soviet activist — and got him fired from the Boston Symphony with a strict "No association" clause: any Symphony employee caught playing in one of Nicholas's string ensembles was to be subject to instant dismissal. No trade unions in his Symphony Orchestra for "Kouss," whose wife had forfeited her enormous fortune to the Revolution!

These Soirees were open to me provided that I never be caught trying to participate in any of the conversations on pain of being sent straight up to bed. So I spent those fabulous smoke-filled evenings, amidst my father's Modern Art and my Mother's fascinating Beautiful Things, listening with all my ears.

Every world problem, political, economic or moral, was settled there amidst swirling conversations in which the most incredible phrases were slung about and the most outlandish and far-fetched opinions were vouchsafed and worked over. Here, no doubt, is where I heard the phrase, "opposed to nationalistic measures." Perhaps if I had been allowed to participate I might have learned how to use some of the phrases shouted so freely.

4. College Radical

When finally I graduated from High School, I had been accepted into Radcliffe College, now an integral part of Harvard University, without the need, thanks to my excellent grades, to take an entrance exam.

My failure to seize the math prize in High School was undoubtedly responsible for my majoring in physics and math at Radcliffe College, from which study I emerged in 1936 with a Phi Beta Kappa (bestowed in my Junior year) and a Summa cum Laude in Physics.

Student Hodee, c. 1932

The most significant development in my life at Radcliffe was not in the scholarship realm. Rather it was my joining, at the end of my Freshman year, the Young Communist League of America. My parents had told me I was free not only to believe as I wished; but to practice those beliefs. After all, this was America, the land of Democracy in Action.

This membership I entered into not out of conviction, but because I had blithely promised to join "later" in order to get their persistent recruiters, all of whom were being graduated, off my back. The girl told me, "Well, if you're joining later, you'd better do it now, because all the rest of us except two are being graduated." There I was, trapped in a lie. But in our family, lying was the ultimate sin. I couldn't admit it, so I joined, and I remember signing the card. It said that I was pledging to work "for a Soviet America." I hadn't the foggiest notion what that was, but I figured I'd find out.

My studies I pursued mechanically, never taking books home, doing my homework in the Library, which taught us deep concentration because I had selected Physics to major in and had no time to listen as the other girls in that library discussed their love lives in juicy detail. I enjoyed mastering the theory of the Physics texts. During those four years, I took all the Physics courses offered, and still found time volunteer as assistant to the Chairman of the Harvard Physics Department, Professor Fred Saunders, in his project "to investigate what makes the Stradivarius a great violin."

I loved working in Harvard's Physics Department sub-basement in the sound-proof room, putting little weights onto a small balance above a wheel of rotating plastic lamina that served as a continuous bow for the $5 Sears fiddle resting in the holder. ("Since we can't afford a Strad," Professor Saunders had quipped, "we'll find out instead what makes a Sears model so bad.") There was one weight that would be a maximum as you made the strings "speak;" but that maximum would occur on another note at another value if you poured carbon dioxide into the body of the instrument. Thus you discovered which tone was due to the vibrating wooden body; which, to the vibrating enclosed body of gas in the violin's gizards.

Despite all this boning, my real education took place from my Sophomore year on in the ranks of the Communists. With my background of naive belief in the truth of democracy, I saw no reason to conceal my new activities. Wasn't this America? But America went to great pains to show me the true nature of its "democracy." It turned out to be democracy only for those willing to conform to all the myths. "Everyone had the same chance to succeed in the United States," went this myth. "And those who did not so succeed, did not because they just couldn't make the grade."

It was an illusion based on a fairy tale, perpetuated by Hollywood, and spread world-wide, where I would encounter it in faraway places many years thereafter.

The organizing of the Radcliffe Communists was put into my hands because the only two others, who had been in the organization longer than I, were either not sufficiently interested (that was one of them) or too scared (that was the other). From iny dream world, I declared that I would do the job. I "came out" on the campus, announcing that I was the Young Communist League here and anyone wanting to know anything about Communism was to "ask me."

Things got a bit livelier in the lunchroom after that. Loud, high-pitched arguments went on among some of the students, most of whom knew more about Communism than I, who knew virtually nothing. I had succumbed to the lie that just "becoming a Communist" made you automatically privy to all their ideas.

When school closed for the summer, the Communists assigned me to neighborhood groups in Cambridge. There, I met people who did know something about real Communism. Most of them were workers, real live ones who worked in places like Hood's

Dairy or in rubber factories that made real Things. Others were Harvard students, like Gene Bronstein and Saul Friedberg. The only other female besides me was a girl named Blanche who was a worker and talked like one, not like a bloody college student.

These people were "studying Marxism." Nobody explained to me that there was a whole science of political economy out there. They assumed that since I was there, I knew all about it. But I was totally ignorant and their jargon left me out in the cold. I did not enjoy not understanding a word of what was being said. Rather than expose my ignorance after having for so many years been a smarty-pants, I kept quiet. Then I went to HQ and said I wasn't fitting in too well in that group; didn't they have something else for me to do?

They did. I was assigned to the American League Against War and Fascism, which had headquarters in downtown Boston, right next to the Anti-Vivisection League. There I met a most remarkable woman, Lisa Trebst, who was assigned by the Party to build this organization aimed at trying to defang advancing fascism. Lisa was a German and a former actress. She had a stern and rockbound sense of duty to the people of the world. Since the salary she was paid for this organizing job was barely enough to cover office expenses, Lisa solved the housing problem by sleeping on the desk at night. She was petite enough to do it. That sense of duty and devotion made big points with me. I wasn't sure I would have had the guts or stamina to do likewise, but I did admire her without reservation.

Later, Lisa was put in charge of the Party Bookstore on Beach Street in downtown Boston. I needed a job, so she hired me and when I began to sell books, she said I was worth more than she. So she paid me $11 a week, while she, the Bookstore manager, continued with her salary of $10 per week.

There weren't too many customers, so I had plenty of time to absorb the contents of a lot of the stock. I read the transcripts of the "Treason Trials" in the Soviet Union, including the American Ambassador's story, "Mission to Moscow," which seemed to back the statements in the transcripts. I couldn't imagine hating a system so badly that you would put ground glass into butter that would be eaten by children and other people. I was impressed.

When school started, I went back to the activities on campus. I went to parties run by the YCL and there I met Milty, my first genuine boyfriend. He was a YCLer, too, but one who knew what communism was all about. I kept asking questions about the myriads of points I didn't understand. Apparently, my questions were very naive, for Milty used to laugh and say, "You're a funny duck. You ask such crazy questions. You need to go to the Workers' School." Oh? What was that, I wondered.

I inquired and enrolled. It was attendance at that school which kept me in Communist ranks for 14 years. I studied Leontiev's "Political Economy," based on Karl Marx's "Capital," as well as Marxian works like "Value, Price and Profit," "Wage Labor and Capital," and Lenin's "The State and Revolution," and "Imperialism, the Highest Stage of Capitalism."

As a student with the free-thinking background in which I had been raised, these studies were a fantastic revelation to me. Here was a whole new world, a world that intellectuals said they were striving to open to ordinary people, workers.

It was years before I knew enough to understand why the Marxists placed so much store on "workers." I had hardly seen such a creature before joining the communists. I knew mostly only intellectuals, businessmen, professionals – and maids, cooks and janitors. And it soon became obvious that my world was a derivative one, floating atop the other, the real, the Marxian-analyzed world of workers. They created the world's goods and were paid only the cost of their own and their family's subsistence while a neat scheme, called Private Ownership of the Means of

Production, placed the real fruits of their labors into the hands of Industry's owners, to do with as they pleased.

With Milty as my boyfriend, I began meeting on a social basis working people who were the real backbone of the Communist Party. I remember a lot of them; how easy it was to talk to them; how they seemed to accept you and like you right away and admit you to their friendship in an earthy, non-frills way. They set up no barriers or artificial conditions. I felt at home there.

5. Digging into Marxism

Once I had got a taste of Marxist theory, there was no holding me, especially after I found out at the Worker's School that the black people of the U.S. had an independent history, one of their own totally removed from that taught us in History classes in school. There we had been taught that most "masters" were "very kind to their slaves" whom Abraham Lincoln freed. I remembered with serious guilt feelings having won the prize in American History in High School - and they had not even told us that there was such a thing as Negro History. I was angry and chagrined.

I set out to learn everything I could find about Negro History. I learned about W. E. B. DuBois, the great Afro-American scholar; I discovered the real role of black people in the building of this country. It was not, I saw, Abraham Lincoln at all who had freed the slaves; it was the slaves themselves, who in concert with allies among people like the Quakers and the Abolitionists, shook the institution of slavery out of our historical tree.

At the end of four years, I was graduated from the august college with a Summa cum Laude. I had already received my Phi Beta Kappa key at the end of my Junior year. I was the only one in that class who went through in four years and got a "Summa." Of the other two who did, one went through in five years and the other, in six. On that basis, I assume I was first in my class. Yet, not a penny could be found, not even a loan, to enable me to return to my "Alte Shmatte," as my classmate Tillie Davis called our college, for graduate study toward a higher degree.

However, at the last minute, they did come up with a Teaching Scholarship to Bryn Mawr College in Physics. It paid a small salary and you worked toward your Master's degree while acting as a Teaching Assistant in their Physics classes.

I accepted this scholarship, having no alternative. That was how I spent one year in graduate school and then a couple of years in Philadelphia and vicinity which again added to my education, though not in Physics.

Now, before taking off for Philly, I had gone to a Left party one evening just after my graduation. There I met a young merchant seaman named Harvey Richards. In very short order, he became my first husband. We eloped to New York City. Then he left his

Harvey Richards, 1940

job on the WPA in Boston, where he had been trying to organize the workers. He was assured that a WPA job of similar rank and value would be awaiting him when he arrived in the Philadelphia area.

We settled in a boarding house, but Harvey's promised job did not materialize. In one swoop, the WPA had defused a "trouble-maker" from their area, sending him to another area which had been warned about him in advance. It was quite a while till he got a job working in a comrade's screen manufacturing factory. Meantime, I was struggling through graduate Physics in the college. There, once again, my real life took place when we set up a Bryn Mawr Branch of the YCL.

The Branch was the idea of a young lady called Arfus. She was a very self-assured, intelligent young person who seemed to know just where she was going. I thought we should just go ahead and set the Branch up. But Arfus said, No, we had to get permission from the Dean of the College. I wasn't too sanguine about that, but she went blithely over to Head Office. In due course, she was back. The Dean said, yes of course we could have a YCL. Only one condition: Don't get a bad press for the college, Arfus had readily agreed to that.

One of the great events for me that came out of this branch came because sometimes we met outside the college. We met in a barn that had been made over into a residence, lived in by a very democratic lady who was Big in the Democratic Party of the state of Pennsylvania but evidently had not yet, despite what I then considered her advanced age, lost her belief in the all-inclusiveness of American Democracy.

Living with her at one such moment, on one of her periodic tours to lecture in the United States, was the great American leftist and writer, staunch defender of the USSR who died in China as a defender thereof, Anna Louise Strong.

I remember the evening we were to meet the great lady, Arfus and I went to wherever it was she was staying (I think it was somewhere in this same stone barn). Ms. Strong was in the shower so we had to wait for her to emerge. At long last, as we held our breath, the bathroom door opened and a large lady with straight white hair around a very pink face, wearing a billowing pink nightie with lace at the shoulders and around the bosom, seemed to stagger toward the bed into which she fell heavily with a kind of grunt and moan.

"My GOD!" I told myself, "are we ever lucky! This woman is obviously dying and if we hadn't got to meet her now, she might not even be around." I couldn't have been in greater error. Years later, when I wrote Anna Louise in China of this moment, she wrote back that she had been soaking in very hot water which had momentarily weakened and flushed her skin that bright pink. Of course, I cannot recall a single word of the subsequent conversation as the great lady lay panting in her bed.

I cannot remember what we did in that Bryn Mawr YCL. It was all ladylike and legal and very soon, the end of the college year came. I was not a huge success in my Physics job. What I had learned at Radcliffe had been all theory with very little practice, and even the practice we did get in was not clearly related to the theory we were learning.

Hence, though nobody ever bothered to inquire why such a "brilliant" student of physics would do such a thing, it is no longer painful, from this 1987 vantage point, to confess that one of the first things I did was to cut a live wire. It was plugged in somewhere in a room below the one where I was working, the wire going down through a hole in the floor.

The result was that I found myself set squarely, suddenly and emphatically on my butt on the floor. The scissors I had used displayed the neatest little holes, half of a rectangle in the middle of each blade.

The Professors were two redheads; one, Head of Department. He was a fat and arrogant man with a long chubby pink face resting in a doughy double chin. He had vapid blue eyes, a breathless way of talking and a very unpleasant body odor. Of course, both he and Dr. Patterson knew I was a "Red." This stupid incident gave them just the opportunity they needed to crystallize their political prejudices by gaining "permission," so to speak, to treat me with contempt. Neither of them ever asked me a single question or offered to help me overcome this not innate weakness. They wanted to and (I see now) succeeded in driving me out of their department.

As a self-designated Marxist, who earnestly believed Marx's dictum that "Theory without practice is sterile; and practice without theory is blind," I should have taken a lesson. The only lesson I learned, however, was that Physics was not for me.

Hence, I cast about for an alternative way of earning money. Through the wife of the Philadelphia YCL Organizer, who was herself a garment worker, I got into a little dress factory. I was required to produce in that first week, at least $10 worth of piecework on the flying sewing machine in order to hold the job. With help from Judy and some of my "fellow" workers, I did it. I did it a second week, too, and might have become a good garment worker and learned the art of sewing.

Alas! The "Recession" of 1937 was upon us and after the second week, the factory joined so many others of the time, closing down, throwing us all out on the street. That gave me a chance to recover from the incredible aches and pains all over my body that those two weeks had created, unaccustomed as I was to the type of bodyset that sewing at top speed all day long demands.

Thereafter, thanks to my experience at the Beach Street Party Bookstore in Boston, 1 got work in the Party Bookstore in Philadelphia, to which city Harvey and I had moved. The store was run by a compact little woman named Nan Pendrell, who had a skinny mustached husband named Ernie. Nan was really kind to me and helped me in every way she could. I seemed to carry around an air of total innocence that made me seem a lot younger than my actual 22 or 23 years.

While working at the Party Bookstore, I was recommended for and accepted at an "Eight Weeks' School" run by the Communists for garment workers, upholsterers - and me. The school was headed by Carl Reeves, a younger son of the famous Ella Reeve Bloor, known as Mother Bloor, a woman of enormous practical experience in industry. I don't remember the lecturer, but he was from one of the nearby colleges. So, I was right at home, because that class of 40 or 50 people was run just like the college classes I was used to: the "professor" lectured at (often boring) length. The students took their notes.

During the introductory lecture, we were told that Party Schools were different than "bourgeois" schools. That was the theory; probably, also the wish. But it isn't what happened. At any rate, on the last day, we were told to do a "critique" of the school. If we had any criticisms, we were assured, we were to express them. Ole literal-minded me! I went home and wrote 20 (count 'em!) hand-written pages in which I criticized the leadership and conduct of the school for not living up to its promise. I passed my essay in with the rest.

In a few days, at the Bookshop, Nan told me, "Now don't get excited, but Carl Reeve is laying for you. He's going to make a monkey out of you in front of that class. But don't let it upset you, now." WHAT! I went to the last class in great dread. I sat through the entire session while everybody else's "critique" was discussed and praised. Not a word about Hodee. They got to the last one and then Carl Reeve stood up.

Without a single reference to anything actually said in my paper, he proceeded to blast me off the earth. What I heard mainly, (and I was to hear it oftener and oftener as the Party got further and further away from the "masses" they were professing to "lead") was that the Party "would not tolerate" any such "attitude" as that shown in my essay.

I remember the guy next to me, an upholsterer named Caleb. During Reeve's harangue, he leaned over and whispered to me, "Boy, oh boy, you'll never catch me criticising this outfit." Exactly! No time whatsoever was allotted to me to rebutt or reply or even to explain what I had actually said. Class was dismissed. The Almighty had spoken! Being young and tender, I went home and cried all night, despite Nan's admonition not to "let it get to me."

I figured my "career" in the Party was at an end. I waited for the axe to fall. One day, I got a summons to appear at the office of Pat Toohey. He was a miner who had had to leave mining because of TB or silicosis, or whatever they do to miners in the pits. He was a cheerful Irishman with freckles, a long pointed nose, a ready grin and a high-pitched voice, his thinning hair combed straight back from his forehead.

I went there, fully expecting to be expelled from the Party, the ultimate disgrace. The office was a dingy upstairs room with long dusty fly-blown windows, a single light bulb hanging into its middle, shadeless. There were wooden benches around the wall and a desk, at which Pat was seated, talking with someone. People moved around doing various things. I was shut up inside myself in a tight ball.

Finally, the person who had been sitting on the rickety cane-bottomed chair got up and moved away. Pat looked over at me and beckoned. Gingerly, I went over and planked myself on the chair.

"So," began Pat at last, as I fidgeted, "You're Hodee Richards."

I admitted the crime.

"You're the one," he continued, "who wrote That Letter to Carl Reeve, right?"

I nodded my head, mutely.

"Well," drawled he, "1 just read it last night for the first time, and guess what?"

I looked up, waiting to hear, What?

"Everything you said in it was correct. Now, what do you think of that?"

Good LORD! I was totally flabbergasted. I simply gasped.

"But you know something else?" he asked, bending toward me.

I raised my eyebrows, still waiting for that Ax.

"You might have convinced Carl of what you said if you'd gone about it in a different way."

He let that sink in and then continued.

"Wasn't there anything in that school that was any good?" he asked me.

I found my voice. "Why, sure," I said, "it was great that it was even held."

"See?" Pat said. "Now, what if you had started your letter by saying things like that and then launched into your criticisms?"

What, indeed!

"You see, young lady," Pat went on, "we have to make the Revolution with the material we have on hand. There are no ideal perfect revolutionaries. I know Carl Reeve. He has his weaknesses. But do you think he is a bad man?"

I shook my head.

"He just finds it hard to take negative criticism - like everybody else," he finished gently. He stood up.

The interview was over. I was immensely relieved - and somehow, chastened. It was a lesson in life from a past master at living it. No wonder everybody loved Pat Toohey.

Later, I found out that directly after the school ended, everybody in the Party leadership except Pat Toohey had been told about how Carl Reeve dealt with that upstart, Hodee Richards. It had been Nan Pendrell and Reva Putnam, wife of the well-known author Samuel Putnam and secretary of the Philadelphia Party, who had conspired to see that Toohey found out.

Driving to a District Party conference, they had started a loud conversation along the lines of, "Wasn't it awful what Carl Reeve did to poor little Hodee Richards?" Pat Toohey was in the same car.

His response was immediate, "What? What? What? What's this and why wasn't I told?" That had been how he finally got to read my totally negative but "correct" effusion.

I can't remember why now, but we left Philadelphia at the end of a year. Harvey and I lived in a room on Spruce Street. The war in Spain was coming to its sad end. Harvey decided that he wanted to volunteer for active service. This was not too long after we were married.

At that point, newly married and anticipating "wedded bliss" and other stereotypical rewards, all my alleged "principles" folded up. I started to cry. There was zero response from my "new" husband. I was determined, I guess, to elicit some kind of response, but he won: I "cried" all night but he never moved nor spoke. He had made his "decision" - and who did I think I was?

We never spoke of this incident. It moved down inside my Being and lodged there like a burr. How could other women be so noble and self-sacrificing? Or more important: why couldn't I? I think that my first reaction was that I was being personally rejected by someone who had only just "accepted" me, so to speak. Had he moved to show some tenderness, some understanding, conceded perhaps that his decision did affect me and that he hoped for my support, even made some political talk for his decision and what he hoped for from me . . . in short, had he reacted humanly, I am sure I could have stood up "as others did."

And the irony of the whole thing is that, had I held my ground, stiff-upper-lipped it, I could have appeared a Heroine, as obviously expected - for the Spanish Government was by then no longer accepting foreign volunteers. Harvey would have been rejected and one less crack would have appeared in the wall of our marriage. Instead, I believe that this incident was the beginning of the end of our marriage, which came in 1946.

Maybe this incident was the reason we left. In any case, we did. We returned to Boston, where I again worked for Lisa in the Party Bookstore on Beach Street.

Harvey and I got an apartment in the West End of Boston, not far from the Charles Street jail where, in 1927, Sacco and Vanzetti had been electrocuted. We had a robbery in our place once, but all the thieves took was food. The neighbors were anything but friendly. But just up the street was Silver's Bakery which made the most mouth-watering delicious-smelling Jewish breads which we bought and ate hot from their ovens.

I remember lying in bed mornings (Harvey had a job working nights; I worked in the Bookshop by day, so we joked that we kept the bed warm without hardly ever seeing one another), imagining myself marching naked through the streets of Boston, bare feet burned or frozen, depending on weather, by having to walk on Street Car tracks . . . all for the crime of being a Jew. I think the Party fostered this sort of fear and trembling with its emphasis always on the negative.

During this time, I joined the nearby Elizabeth Peabody House, a neighborhood house that had a Drama Group I joined. There, I appeared as Mrs. Disraeli (looking rather like George Washington in my white wig) in the well-known play, "Disraeli." The only reason I mention this is because the part of the femme fatale in that play was played by Ruth Roman, then 17 and already married. She had the whole cast in the palm of her hand. Years later, on the strength of that moment in life, I remember visiting her in a hotel room when she was appearing in a play at a local theater. By then she had become ten years my junior instead of five; and someone had taken out her distinctive and attractive little overlapping eye teeth and replaced them with a nice, non-offensive set of falsies. Those teeth had seemed to me when we were momentarily thrown together in person as a large part of her ingenuous charm. However, she did make it to Name Status in Glamour City, with or without her own front teeth.

Left politics were very rough in those days. Longshoremen fighting to organize a union on the docks of Boston got tossed through plate glass windows. We had come through the depths of a world-wide depression and begun to live under the increasing euphoria of Franklin Delano Roosevelt's measures that saved the "American Way" for the American ruling class, which repaid him by hating his guts. They couldn't overcome their Herbie Hoover legacy that the only way to make a profit was to squeeze the devil out of the workers. But following the horrors of the Great Depression, the workers weren't having any, thank you, and it was either Roosevelt's way or the possibility that even American workers would join the world-wide trend to Revolution and horrors like "overthrowing the Government."

The Party leadership at Boston HQ were under pressure from the Martin Dies Committee. War was raging in Spain. Young men whom I had met in the YCL at Harvard and in Cambridge, good guys like Gene Bronstein and others, volunteered service in Spain, most serving in the Abraham Lincoln Brigade. The inspiring concept of "international solidarity" took on flesh and blood meaning . . . many of these guys died trying to save the world from fascism, putting their bodies on the line at its leading edge in Spain.

People began to leave the District for other areas. In fact, there were so many that finally, Phil Frankfeld, Party Boss in Boston, had, one day at the dingy Party headquarters, made a loud threat relating to "the next person who asks for a transfer out of this district."

Phil Frankfeld was a man who yelled at others. With his round fat face, beetling black eyebrows and an ever-present cigar butt jutting from one side of his wide mouth with its widely spaced big teeth, he had an air of The Gangster about him. He had a wonderful wife, Fanny, who (not unexpectedly) later left him. If you wanted to move from one district to another in the Communist Party, you had to apply for and be granted an official "transfer" which you then presented to the Secretary of the new area. This is not as strange as it sounds in an era when the Government was infiltrating Party ranks with its finks.

It would be nice to believe that we were really such a threat to said Government's existence. I don't believe we were – and I believe the Government didn't think so, either. Infiltration was just one of their (successful) strategies for scaring the rest of the populace away from the Party . . . which, in turn, convinces me that the Party had something definite and positive to offer the American people, which, some day, I am going to try to name, and, in a constructive way, describe why they failed.

Well, Harvey was from Oregon. He hated the East Coast, constantly referring to its - to me - gorgeous scenery as "scrub brush and foothills." He was dying to get back to the Great Wild West, whence he had come. As for me, frankly, I was having the jitters and nightmares about being paraded down Main Street in the altogether with my head shaved, like the women in Nazi Germany, when fascism took over, as the Party was freely predicting, unless "their way" was followed by the majority.

So it came to pass that, one day, we applied for a transfer. And guess what? WE were that "next person" to whose application for a transfer Phil Frankfeld had vowed, and now gave - a denial.

It didn't take us a minute to decide what to do. In equally short order, we left the East Coast.

6. The West Coast

Harvey persuaded my parents to cut loose with bus fare and we set off for the Golden West on Greyhound Bus. We traveled night and day but I could hardly sleep on the bus. By the time we reached Salt Lake City, I felt ready to die. So, we stopped off and got a good night's sleep. Then off we went again, into Oregon.

There we met Harvey's two half brothers. Then on we went, down the Coast in another bus, toward the Mecca of the West, San

Hodee and Harvey
San Francisco, 1940

Francisco, where Harvey's sister Katherine, her husband of the time, Jack Wilbur, and their two children lived.

We stayed with Katherine for a few weeks. During our very first full day, I discovered that "snails" in this part of our country, were not necessarily slimy animalcules, but pastry. I also found out that one very active form of local wild life was the flea, which fed royally off my person. And one day, I outraged Harvey when, at my first sniff of eucalyptus trees, I asked, "What is that medicine smell?" Medicine, indeed! I fell in love with San Francisco and its white houses and white cars.

It was 1940.

We had come into this area under a political cloud: two self denominated Communists without a transfer.

After we left Katherine's apartment by the panhandle of Golden Gate Park, we got an apartment in Arguello Blvd., right at the corner where street cars then made their screeching turns night and day.

I decided I wanted to have a child. Seven months went by, but I showed no signs of pregnancy. I began to get really uptight about it. By then, I had found my lovely gynecologist, Frances Foster, mother of three or four kids herself. She said she had some delightful "treatments" planned for me that would make me conceive. I didn't like the sound of her promise nor did I like the gleam in her eye.

However, Nature helped me to thwart her plans. I came down with pneumonia. I was so sick that for the one and only time in my life, I was physically unable to raise my head off the pillow at the doctor's command to do so. I went to the hospital, where they put me on the new "sulfa" drugs which had begun to save the lives of GI's in the European theater of war.

It was while I was lying so ill, just before I went into the hospital, that I received word of my father's death at the age of only 57 of stomach cancer. Now I recalled how, during all those years of the Great Depression, the No-Income Year, and other bad times, he had come home from work and gone straight upstairs to his bathroom, to vomit noisily. This went on week after week. First it happened on Tuesdays; later it changed to Thursdays. My Dad took to drinking acidophilus milk.

I had been away so far and so long, I had not been aware of the direction this had taken. My Dad's death, much like his life, was far removed from me. I realized that, regardless of our talks together, we had never been close at all. In fact, sad to relate, we had been virtual strangers.

Sam Waldstein c. 1941

Life had to go on and mine did. When I got home from the hospital, I asked Frances if I should continue to use my contraceptives. She said, "No, you won't get pregnant till I do my number on you." Famous last words. The time I spent lying around convalescing, together with the absence of stress, since I "wasn't going to get pregnant anyway," made the difference.

We moved into the Sunset District of San Francisco, out "in the Avenues," and in due course, Steffen, my first child, was born after only five hours of labor. I did not experience his birth since Frances had me put under with one of those drugs that leaves you conscious while it's going on but without memory when it is over.

I wanted to nurse the child, but the pediatrician we had hired before the birth, put my son on a bottled formula when my milk didn't flow from the first in rivers. After that, the child wouldn't even bother to suck on such a miserable source of nourishment and I immediately panicked.

I phoned Frances from the hospital. Her husband, a labor lawyer, was off in Kansas City at a Labor Convention; her kids were away at their summer home. She came and got me out of the hospital

Harvey and Hodee with first born son, Steffen. 1942.

and took me home with her. There, she stuck the formula in the fridge, and let the child get so hungry that the first time she brought him to me and he smelled that good Mother's milk, he didn't just nurse; he snarled a bestial snarl and bit the hell out of me.

I never did have much milk, but Frances said it made up in quality for what it lacked in quantity. I nursed him for a full nine months. After that, he never would take a rubber nipple. He went straight from the breast to a cup.

He turned out to be allergic to everything except four veggies and three fruits and Frances sent me to a lady doctor to see what to do about it. She put him onto pure soy bread, for which I was told to go to a specific Health Food Store. I had a Thing against Health Food Stores, like everyone else at the time; but for my first born, I made the noble sacrifice.

Hodee, Harvey, Norma (Harvey's mother)
and baby Steffen. San Francisco, 1943.

Meantime, Harvey and I worked diligently at again being accepted in the Party. We reported to Headquarters and told our story of how we came to be present without a transfer. We were given a probation period. I remember a Party functionary in the office on Haight Street, Emma. She advised me that my best bet for becoming a proper Communist was to become a proletarian. I should, she advised, get myself a job in a factory.

Well, I didn't tell her that I'd already done that for two whole weeks as a garment worker in Philadelphia. I did not agree with the lady about becoming an artificial proletarian. My background was what it was and I had the nerve to think (and was later proven correct) that that background gave me something special to offer The People. Maybe I wouldn't write that definitive book my Dad had urged me to do; but I sure as hell could and loved to work with words. In that field, I felt confident, I had something to offer. So, that was the direction in which I set out to make my contribution to the Party.

Meantime, the District Secretary had changed. The new one was Steve Nelson, the hero of the Abraham Lincoln Brigade in Spain. Steve was a wonderfully human person who had offered his life for what he believed in. He had passed the final test of sincerity in those beliefs. He tended to think the best of everyone, but was definitely nobody's fool.

But what gave me my direction was that the Daily PEOPLE'S WORLD, West Coast equivalent of the New York DAILY WORKER, advertised one day for volunteers to help with short-handedness on the staff. I immediately showed up.

I was ushered into a tiny office. A long, lanky, somewhat swarthy but freckled man with curly blond hair and permanently raised blond eyebrows asked me to sit down. He said he was John Pittman, editor of the paper. He asked me if I could write. I assured him that I was a writer. He gave me an article and told me to take it home arid do a rewrite on it.

When I took it back the next day, "Pitt" looked at it and said, "OK, come in." Again we went into his office.

"Young lady," he said in the slowest drawl I'd ever listened to, "how would you like to cover the war news?"

I assured him I would love to. World War II was in full swing and the Soviet Union was now "on our side." Pitt showed me what to do: take the morning war news in the "capitalist press" and match it against the big map on the wall; move the colored pins around so we could see where The Front was and what it was doing. Then, write up the result as tersely as possible.

"General," he drawled, "take a name. After all, a woman can't write war news."

Some years before, I had pretended to my college class mates who were so reluctant to be known as Reds that, indeed, my family, too, were "just furious" about my working with the American League against War and Fascism. (No doubt that was why my Dad always took me to their meetings and picked me up after they were over.) At that time, I had followed the custom of "taking a Party name." Mine was Linda Shepard.

Now, as Pitt made his request, I took that name back, but with a slight difference.

"OK," I told him, "I'll be L. C. Shepard."

That was the name under which I wrote war news for two years or so. I even did a series in the paper, called, "Ships of the Line for the Layman," the information out of some popular book of the moment which described Navy ships at length.

The "difference" about my new "Party name" was that if you say those initials, L.C., reasonably fast, it sounds just the same as if you'd said, "Elsie." That tickled me for years. A woman was writing war news.

In 1944, as World War II was coming to its end, my second son was born, Paul Richards. This birth was faster and easier than the first one: it took 90 minutes from the first pain to the baby and we just barely made it to the hospital. At that time, we were living in the Potrero district, in a big wooden Victorian house owned by one Mrs. Moglia. Mrs. Moglia was a rabid fan of Thomas Dewey's. During the 1944 election, Harvey and I campaigned vigorously for FDR. Mrs. Moglia's response was to turn up her powerful radio to top volume about 2 or 3 in the morning so that sleep was literally impossible. We moved.

By now, Harvey was a machinist in the shipyards of San Francisco. He was exempted from the draft by fatherhood. We got a place to live at the edge of McLaren Park in a housing project for service men and women or for "war workers." It was a nice, clean place with everything in concrete and tile, small but adequate. We hired a woman to take care of the kids, because we both worked.

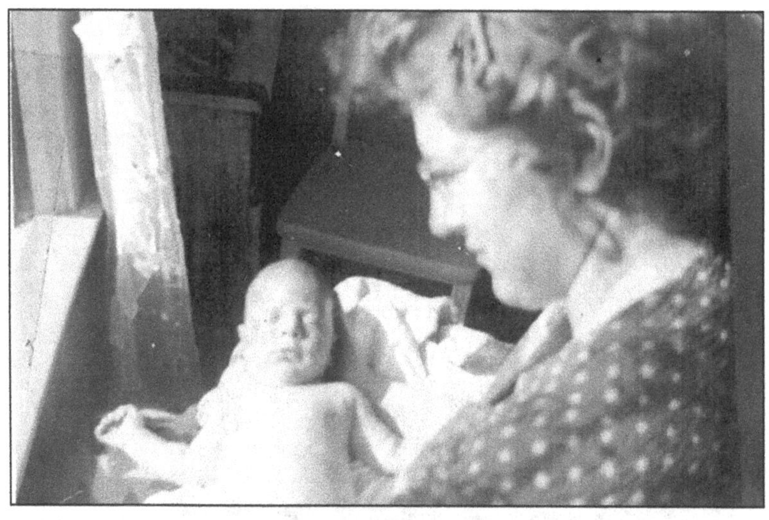

Hodee with infant Paul. 1944

I was a recognized writer, writing under my own name once the war and my "news coverage" of it ended. I had been making a study of the great Thaddeus Stevens and the entire Reconstruction Period of American History and had some columns about him. I had also gotten into the "Woman Question" hot and heavy.

I don't particularly recall the exact sequence of events, but Pitt stopped being the editor of the PW and went to Chicago to write for the Chicago DEFENDER. Harrison George became the new editor, a laconic, red-faced man with a wry sense of humor who always wore a battered hat and set great store by "colonics". Vern Smith was the foreign editor.

On the PW Staff I was forever a shit-disturber. I remember one battle royal that raged for a few months over whether or not the "People's Paper" should run cheesecake, the display of women's bodies unrelated to text and just for the hell of it. I said it had no place in our press. In short order, all the women on the paper with the exception of one, were on "my" side; all the men, again, except one, on the other. The letters to the editor became heated.

Back row: Harvey holding Paul, Jack Wilbur, Norma Richardson, Hodee, in front, Karen Wilbur, Kyle Wilbur and Steffen. San Francisco, 1945

I don't know how it came out but can guess. Adam Lapin, by then editor, showed me a copy of the New York DAILY WORKER, with cheesecake displayed. "See," says he triumphantly, "the WORKER uses cheesecake." I looked at the poor man with contempt and spat out, "That doesn't prove it's right; not to me. All it proves is that those guys need education, too." I won't forget the totally nonplussed look that elicited from Adam (may he rest in peace).

I guess they got sick of my constant stirring up around there and so when Al Richmond, the peppery ex-longshoreman, became editor, he took me off the writing end. He called me in and said they were going to make me "Circulation Manager." They said it was no good having even the best writing in the paper's columns if there weren't enough people to support its existence. That made sense to me. I accepted the job. I thought they were serious.

It was during my brief stay in this job on the paper that I met George Edwards. He was the West Oakland Party Organizer and a struggle that he had initiated was in progress, being reported in the "PW." That was the "Safeway Picket Line." George had started this struggle which soon embraced the entire neighborhood and many of its organizations, led by the redoubtable and highly respected Reverend Johnson. The struggle was to force Safeway to hire at least one black cashier. Safeway had vowed that they would never, no never, be that foolish.

The "PW" played an active and honorable role in mobilizing people for that fight. There was a daily picket line that covered that store's front door and its business slid down to near-zero. The famous "A" train that used to cross the San Francisco Bay over the Bay Bridge on railroad tracks long since removed, passed right by that corner. That's how I first saw the picket line.

After many months, the struggle was won, but not before George had had to oppose the entire West Oakland Party leadership. They told him, "OK. You've made your point. You've shown the people of that neighborhood where the Party stands, but we can't spend forever fighting a big corporation like Safeway. Directives for other work are coming in from New York."

George said nothing, but he took a trip to Los Angeles to see Pettis Perry, whom everyone called Pete, a black Party official in that city, who I believe was on the Party's National Committee. He said he told Pete what was going on and Pete asked him what he wanted to do. George said he thought it was very important to carry the struggle through to a successful conclusion. He felt the end was near; that Safeway would be forced to give in; and that the entire neighborhood around that store was waiting to see what the Party

Hodee and George Edwards,
1948. Photo by Jake Price

would do. He said he wanted to stick with the fight that he had started till it ended one way or the other. So Pete said, "OK. Then do it."

George was right. Safeway did give in. Then it came time to negotiate the actual settlement. Reverend Johnson came to George and said he thought that, for actually gaining what they had fought for, it would be best if the Party was not sent to head the negotiations with Safeway directly. He felt this would stick so badly in the Safeway craw that the whole struggle would be lost. George felt that everyone in the neighborhood and for miles around knew who had started, supported and organized that struggle, so he agreed to the Reverend's proposal and suggested that the Reverend himself, who was well known and completely respected, should head the committee.

This concession got George no high marks with the local Party leadership who accused him of selling out. It seemed to me that the difference between them was that between a man of the people, who moved among the people and knew what they were thinking and a group of Big Theorists who knew what was best for everyone, especially for the People.

So George made way for Reverend Johnson and Safeway hired a black clerk. This, I believe, was the first time a giant corporation in the U.S. had been brought to its knees by people power, persistence and policy. Yet the victory was reported on Page 3 of the PEOPLE'S WORLD, in a very off-hand report.

By that time, I was working with George Edwards as Circulation Manager of the paper, and when I delivered a bundle of the paper that carried that Page 3 story, I remember his looking at it and silently throwing the paper down. He didn't say a word, so I did. I told him I thought it was outrageous that "our" paper saw this tremendous people's victory as worthy only of a laconic story on an inside page. George let loose, then, venting his own wrath and disappointment.

That was the beginning of our relationship. He was amazed to find a white person who "knew so much about Negro History." And I found myself deeply attracted to his big masculinity and his dynamism and personal charm. I began to see more and more of him, always - of course - as Circulation Manager. I fought against recognizing the attraction, but probably not too hard.

This was only possible because, "back at the ranch," as they say, my marriage to Harvey had been going blah for some time.

The loosening of ties between us began before I was working, because I remember studying daily in that project home while Harvey worked at the shipyards. I was planning to write a comparison between Andrew Johnson and Harry S. Truman and their respective political periods, their respective roles in our history. I had already begun the reading and was making a card file of notes. I was really impressed with the similarities: Andrew Johnson, the tailor; Harry Truman, the haberdasher . . . each coming to power on the death of a historical giant at the end of definitive wars...

I always tried to set a time limit for the study so I could stop and prepare dinner, look after my small sons, take care of the house, etc. I guess, one day, it got too fascinating and I was still at it when Harvey showed up and I still, as he so delicately phrased it later, "had my nose in a book instead of rolling on the bed playing with my children." This dismal failure of mine, he assured me, proved to him that I did not love the children. In short, I was a Bad Mother.

I got past that somehow, though the accusation stuck in my craw. My indignation went inward, even too far for me to see right away. I swallowed the flip and mundane judgement and suffered with it for some time. We never discussed it: I heard his pronounced sentence and, apparently at the time accepting it as correct, ate it and got spiritually sick on it. Harvey was not a man for discussion. He makes pronunciamentos.

At the same time, in about November of 1946, my connection with the PW came to an abrupt and unpleasant end. During my first few months of acting as "Circulation Manager," I had given the matter of increasing the paper's readership a lot of thought. I came up with Plans. I submitted one. They told me, "Yes, that's fine, but right now, the Party is asking us to..." whatever it was. Often three months of such incidents, it suddenly came through to me that the job as Circulation Manager was a big joke. I was expected to be a rubber stamp to whatever "they" in their infinite wisdom decided. Wow! Steam began to snort from my nostrils. I wrote a letter to Al Richmond, in which I basically said that they never would have treated a man as they were treating me.

In nothing flat, I found myself in an office with the door closed and three males seated in a row confronting me. They were Al Richmond, Leo Barroway and Harry Kramer (I think Harry was the paper's Financial Manager; I forget what Leo's job was). Anyhow, after a due settling in, Al Richmond began.

Said he, "We have read your recent pontification..." and went on. I didn't hear him, though. Inside my head, went the word "pontification." "Pontiff?" The Pope? What the hell does that mean? when I came to, Al was saying that in their august opinion, I should either bring charges of "male chauvinism," as "sexism" was then called in our circles, or resign from the paper, "after the circulation drive concludes, of course."

I wanted very much to bring such charges, but the Party was and continues to be run - like everything else in this world - by men. I had a blinding flash of myself being ground to mincemeat in the machine of their "formal charges." No thanks. So like a big fool, I stayed on till the circulation drive ended.

7. After Communism

This was the start of a new era in my life. For the first time in my adult life, I was no longer officially connected with the Party or any of its arms or limbs. I was strictly on my own, like the rest of the ordinary population, and in need of a job. I began to look for work in the Real World.

On top of that, my family had broken up. After first moving out, I had soon convinced Harvey to move out instead and let me live with the children. Soon, it became too inconvenient having to "Take the A Train" to Oakland every time I wanted to see George. I began to try to figure some way so that I and the kids could move to Oakland to be near or with him.

Harvey had hired a woman named Vivian to take care of the house and kids while he was at work. She lived in. I kept her on when I moved back in, a decision I had cause to regret in short order.

Vivian was the daughter of an alcoholic who was perhaps a prostitute at the same time. I recall her horrendous story of how her mother broke her of bed-wetting at age seven: she sent the child out to play wrapped in the bed sheet she had wet the night before.

When she came to our place, the girl was pregnant. Her child was born on April 5 of that year, and I named her. Vivian wanted to call her April; in my infinite wisdom, I suggested Avrille, the French name for the same month.

George was smitten by Vivian at once. I didn't know it because he was an old hand at concealing such things: some kindly women in Party ranks tried to tell me that I was just one in a long female line awaiting attention from Mr. George. But I refused to believe that. I was in love with him. And didn't he say he loved me?

I can hardly believe, now, how ignorant I was about human relationships. I also know now that what I had mistaken for deep love was only what I came to call "The Lure of the Unattainable."

It wasn't too long till George, too, left his various positions of leadership with the Party. He told me they were trying to manipulate him behind his back, probably because of our relationship which was causing a lot of uproar in the Party. The comrades, especially the female ones, began to find all sorts of "chauvinism" in my everyday conduct. It was after I realized that this was just their own very real chauvinism peeking out at my expense that I quit going to meetings. Let them get on with Party business.

Having left such positions, George, too, had to look for work. Through friends he got into the Laborers' Union in Oakland and was soon doing construction work. With his great physical strength and easy-going manner – he was a man's man just as much as he was a lady's man – he was soon laying sewer pipe and doing road construction. He became an expert on the making of good lasting concrete.

It was in 1946 that the way cleared for me and George to live together. I started divorce proceedings against Harvey. Not too long before then, I had had to ask Vivian to move. I can't remember the circumstances. Some time later, in a candid moment, she told me that she found my breathless hanging on whether or not George would phone me really silly. She was right, and I paid heavily for this silliness of mine.

I moved out of the project and George and I moved in with a mutual friend who had a house on E. 19th Street. That was Eleanor. Her son Mike became fast friends with my two boys; his age was just between the two. However, it took a year before I got my court date and the divorce; another year before it became final.

George and Paul, at the park,
c. 1947

Vivian moved, too, all right. She took a room with one of my dear friends, Lillie Bell, who had a big house on MacArthur Blvd, in Oakland where she took in comrades to make ends meet. This made it easier for George to start and continue his secret relationship. Lil was just as naive as I was about such things. Meantime, I had been so anxious to have a child with George. I told myself I was madly, madly in love with him. I have no memory whatever of events that happened in those lost years, a horrible time of my life because, basically, I did not really know what was going on in my relationship. I knew it was awful; I didn't know what to do about it. I couldn't believe that the man didn't love me; and really, I think he did. Numbers of my good friends think so, too. That wasn't the problem.

There was not only the man-woman Thing to stand between the two of us; in our case, there was a big cultural difference. Despite my academic knowledge of Negro History, now called Black History, I had not lived it as my black brothers and sisters had. I could not, for example, even begin to understand beforehand, when it would have mattered, the role that sexuality had played in slave life in Black History. That was why I could think it funny or cute to blame George publicly for my failure to conceive a child with him.

I would tease him in public. He never let on that he was resenting my stupid actions, and obviously, I was not too sensitive to his feelings. He took his revenge by strengthening the liaison with Vivian. I, of course, remained in ignorance of the whole thing for some time.

My divorce became final in April of 1948. Two days later, George and I set out for the state of Washington to get married. In those days, "mixed" marriages were illegal in the Great State of California. Harry Bridges, the tough Longshoremen's Union leader, was the one who broke that up when he deliberately married a Japanese woman in the sacred state and they couldn't do anything about it. But I was no Harry Bridges.

George and I were married in Vancouver, Washington, with two Party officials as witnesses. I had been ecstatic, little dreaming of the years ahead of me with the man, 17 of them spent in misery.

The relationship wasn't based on reality from the beginning, so, it's amazing that it lasted 21 years. I do remember feeling deeply privileged when George had begun taking me around, introducing me to his friends, most of whom were "black," by U.S. definition. I found wonderful lifetime friends among them. They had plenty of hang ups from the kind of life that had been forced on them (that is, different from white hang ups) but they were warm and real, forthright and colorful in an emotional sense. I am forever grateful to George for letting me into his world, from which I can never again be expelled and yet in which I do not belong and do not really live.

At first, we continued to live with Eleanor and Paul. Then we got a place of our own in West Oakland, the city's "black" neighborhood. I think it was during this time, too, that I began to teach evening and weekend classes in Marxism. I taught the basic classes, like "Wage Labor and Capital," "Value Price and Profit," "The State and Revolution," "Imperialism, the Highest Form of Capitalism."

In my classes a young black man began to attend, Tim Evans. He was a clean-cut young fellow with a round face, round gold-rimmed spectacles. He had lots of questions about the material I was teaching. I tried to the best of my ability to answer them. I liked Tim. He was always so pleasant and seemingly respectful of Teacher, which gave a velvet edge to his questions.

It was there too that, finally, George had to tell me of Vivian's pregnancy. He wanted me to divorce him so he could marry her. Oh, he did, did he? Well, at last a weapon in my hands! I refused. I urged that she have the baby in my name. She refused. My misery deepened. I went about my daily chores at home and on whatever job I may have had, like an automaton.

We got a chance to rent a house in a rustic setting in the town of Niles, so we moved out of West Oakland.

In Niles, we lived in the little house next to a fine couple who had a big strawberry patch, pigs and two ugly white bulldogs, who looked a lot worse than they were. George was still absent, night after night. I would sit at the window as my sons slept, waiting and waiting for my husband to come home. It's hard to believe as I write of it now, but there were years of similar anguish.

Then, one day in June (it was 1950), he told me he was "going on a business trip with Okie." Okie was a fellow from Oklahoma who was in construction work with George.

I didn't like the idea of his being gone for the weekend again, but there was nothing I could do about it. So off he went. He had said he'd be back Sunday night. Of course, Sunday night came and went without his presence. It was a condition I found I could not stand.

I called Okie's house and asked his wife "if Okie had got back from his business trip yet." There was a pause and then Mrs. Okie quietly announced that Okie hadn't gone anywhere; had been there the whole time. My heart sank. And suddenly, I knew where George had been and why and what would happen when he arrived. He was bringing his child by Vivian home - to ME!

Sure enough. He showed up after work on Monday. And there was the baby, on the front seat, screaming her poor heart out. The back of the car was full of dirty diapers and used nursing bottles. There was a letter of "instructions" from the mother, who signed herself, "Maxine." I knew of no Maxine. George had nothing to say, not a word. I recall rejoicing that the child was female, for had it been a boy, I knew George would be gone. I was worried about my ability to care properly for my two sons without a man's help and influence around.

The kids greeted the new arrival with unbridled joy. "Oh, BOY!," exclaimed Pauli, the younger, leaping off the few porch steps, "a BABY!" From the start, the boys accepted this girl child as their own. They taught her to talk, to walk. They loved her. It was great.

The first night, of course, I was not prepared to handle two-month-old babies. The poor child slept in a huge carton that was hanging about from some grocery trip. She screamed the whole night, for which I couldn't blame her. I was wrapped up in my own misery and vast humiliation. The child was truly beautiful, with long curling black eyelashes and eyes like liquid brown pools, as in novels. Here was the child I had wanted. I demanded to name her, not to accept the silly name on the birth certificate. George agreed to anything, just so I'd keep her.

I tried to ignore the heartache and did my beat for the child, but I fear I wasn't very good at it. Not at all like Bea Dadson in Ghana, who at different times took in 13 children allegedly fathered by her M.P. husband and raised them as her own, setting up their own school for them and whatever else they required. I was locked into Western prestige patterns and this sure wasn't good for mine. Yet my acceptance of the child earned me real high marks with friends among black and other party women (except the wives of Party officials, of course).

For me, the Western woman, it was hard. Especially after I finally found out who the mother was. This came about when the newsboy came to the door for his money and George was asleep.

Steffen, Paul, Hodee, George
and Louee, 1952. Photo by Jake Price

I had to rifle his pockets for some money. Along with the money was a letter, which I promptly read. It was as mushy as could be and signed "Vee. " I knew the handwriting well. He got no more sleep that day.

Eventually, we moved back to Oakland. First, we separated, each of us living in a separate place, each in a room. I worked in San Leandro as a "skip tracer," a job that lasted only nine months because the boss said I was "too soft on these dead-beats." During that summer, we had no place for the boys. They spent the summer in Chinese Camp with dear friends who, without blinking an eye, took them and kept them till we could again care for them. After two years of this, one Fall, we came together again.

At that time, it was almost impossible for black people to get decent housing. We moved to various places in East Oakland. I would go and rent a place. We would move in; the rents would promptly be raised out of reach and we'd go through it all again. We lived in four different places on East 19th Street.

Our stay at the top of the hill opposite St. Anthony's Park was the worst. George kept seeing Vivian, though he continued to deny it. He was gone more and more often. I hated for it to rain because he couldn't work when it rained and he would just disappear. Later he claimed he was playing cards at the Labor Temple in Oakland. Some of the time, sure.

Later, when Louee, as she came to be called (I had named her Eva for an Aunt of George's and Lou for fun, so she was Eva Lou) was seven years old, I went to a lawyer friend and arranged to and did adopt Louee as my own.

Vivian still hadn't given up on trying to break up my marriage. I figured that was my reward for helping her when she needed help before her daughter Avrille was born. She made "conditions" for agreeing to the adoption. I said she could take me to court; no conditions. I had learned that she had married a Georgia cracker whom she met in some bar and I was sure she would not really be anxious to let him know she had a "black" baby (a fact in which I gloried). So in due course, the adoption went through.

I didn't tell my daughter about this. All the books on bringing up baby said you only answer questions when a child asks them. Now what child is going to ask that? Well, mine did one horrible day in Sweden some four years later. But we'll get to that. Besides, I thought she surely knew: she had been seven years old when she appeared in a little courtroom with the judge who was deciding whether or not to agree that I could adopt her.

Meantime, my search for jobs went on. I can tell you how the Social Security system really works. For two years, I went from job to job. Each job lasted exactly 90 days, the time required for you to pass your probation period and be hired. After the first couple of times, I began to feel cynical about it. As soon as I started on a job, the person who had hired me would assure me I had nothing to worry about; my work was among the best they had ever had there. Un-hunh! And, sure enough, in 90 days, bingo! "Something in your references does not quite check out," or some other bullshit. Never once did they say to me, "Get outta here, ya doity Red." No, it was all polite and comme il faut, and thus, twice as deadly as open warfare, when you can see the enemy's ugly face.

I finally got a job with Henry Kaiser's Headquarters in Oakland. That lasted two years. I was hired to build and maintain a clipping service for the top ten executives of the Kaiser Empire, all of whom had offices in that building (not the current one; the building before that). That included "The Old Man," Henry Kaiser himself.

They were delighted with my work. So was I. I read 50 daily and Sunday newspapers and about 100 weekly and monthly periodicals and all I had to do was find and clip out and file retrievably anything that dealt with the Kaiser "empire" or any portion thereof. Every evening, I would prepare a set of clip sheets bearing the cuttings of that day, which I would run upstairs to the penthouse where all the Greats hung out.

That job gave me a chance to read stuff I otherwise would never even have seen. I loved it. They gave me an office of my own and I worked as happily as a little lark.

My past experience convinced me that they knew who I was. But they didn't care if I was a Red. In my solitary office, I had little contact with other workers in the building. And Kaiser wasn't afraid of Reds. He had a more realistic view of their actual power than did the Government and its satellites in industry. So, what got me fired off that job was something else, which may come as a revelation about the great Henry Kaiser.

I had joined their Health Plan, Kaiser Hospital, when my job became "permanent." Now, one day, they asked me if I wouldn't like to put my husband on it too; he was eligible. I thought that would be Jim dandy.

So I applied for him, too. Under "race"- which was then a required bit of information - I marked "N." The secretary from the top office came flying in to mine one morning and said, "Oh, Mrs. Edwards, you've made a mistake on your application. " She laid the thing in front of me and pointed to that "N." I looked at the child. "That's not a mistake," I said. There was a big pause. "It's not?" she echoed. "Right," I confirmed. It wasn't two weeks later before the job was "eliminated for economic reasons." I was out on my uppers again.

Years later, in Ghana, an Afro-American with whom George became friendly, Emerson McDowell, a master electrician, was working for Henry Kaiser at a housing project being done for the Ghana Government. Mac was going with an English girl and at some company party or other, he introduced her to a couple of the Kaiser executives with whom everything in that country was on a buddy-buddy basis. He told them he was going to marry Phyllis.

Not long afterward, they called him in and told him that if he did marry Phyl, it would cost him his job. Mac told us about it. "Can you imagine that, here in Ghana?" he screamed. Of course, he married her. And, by gum, he was fired forthwith. So I know it was not George's imagination when he suggested to me that there were no "economic reasons" why I had no job at Kaiser, despite the "delight" of the execs, with my work. As usual, he was right on the button.

Well, after Kaiser gave me the boot in 1952, I was interviewed for another job. This was with Moore Business Forms, which then had a manufacturing plant in Emeryville, California. The young guy who interviewed me was boyish and blond. He seemed easy-going and ingenuously informed me that he had just celebrated his 30th birthday. I was 37, but was afraid that after 35 you didn't have a chance in the job market, so was passing for 34.

Ed was looking for someone to whom he could entrust his department, which, called The Standards Department, was actually the Time Study Department; he had other fish he wanted to fry. He knew from talking to me that at least the lights were on upstairs, so he hired me.

He tested me by asking me to revamp the Department files. It was a great chance to learn about the operation and I enjoyed it as I accomplished the task. I was on the usual 90-day probation. "Got anything else for me?" I would ask cheerfully, bursting into the main office when my own work ran out. That didn't go over in industry. But I had never really held a job in industry; I'd worked in the Party, where zeal in doing your job was expected. When I applied the same zeal to this job, everyone figured that I was "brown-nosing." Objectively, I understand now, it made Ed want me to stay. But that isn't why I did it; I just didn't know any better at the time. Since our little family needed the income, I wanted to stay, of course, but I wouldn't have thought I needed to kow-tow to get or keep a job. I thought my abilities spoke loudly enough for themselves.

The end of my first 90 days was approaching. I could feel it breathing down my neck. I tried not to think of it. Then, one evening after work, as I flew through the front door with the rest of the released wage slaves, two men stepped in beside me and one of them flashed his ID card at me. FBI! "Oh, hell," was my first thought. "I'll be late getting home again."

I can't remember what these guys looked like because my memory pictures them in snap-brimmed fedoras and belted trench coats "just like in the movies." They asked me to come and sit with them in their car, parked nearby. They (surprise, surprise!) wanted to talk to me.

I stepped into the back seat of the car, while they got into the front seats. I knew quite well that the place was bugged and that a tape would be running, but honestly, I didn't give a damn. I still remained soothed by my mother's childhood assurances that I had a right to believe as I choose.

"OK, fellas," I say as openers, "what do you want with me? I have to get home and cook supper for my family."

"Well," drawled one of them, "we understand that you know a lot about Marxism-Leninism. How would you like to come up to our office and tell us about it?"

I could hardly credit my ears.

"Come off it, guys," I pleaded. "Do you think I am an idiot or something? I told you I have to go home. Now, just tell me what you want and I'll tell you if I am going to give it to you and we can all go home."

"What would you say," began the other one, "if we told you that we have documentary proof that Stalin's government really did give money to the Communist Party of the United States?"

"I understand," I answered, "that one of the major industries of the FBI is manufacturing documents."

They exchanged a glance.

"How do you explain the fact that a lot of Jewish people are leaving the Communist Party?"

"I can't help it," I said, "if the Party doesn't carry out its own program."

Then they asked me the same thing about "Negroes." I gave them the same answer.

More went on in that vein that I have fortunately forgotten. But then, one of them asked me, "How come the Communist Party went underground not so long ago?"

I got up to leave, reaching for the door handle. As I did so, I said, in exasperated tones, "For the same reason that you guys are in the FBI: You've all seen too many Hollywood movies."

I went home and told George what had happened. I said I thought I should go report this to the Party. He advised strongly against any such move: "You stay away from those people," he cautioned. But I have mules in my ancestry somewhere. I thought it would be "the right thing to do," since I had nothing particularly against the Party and they might want the info.

Accordingly, I sought out an old friend. I told her what had happened. Her reaction rather startled me. She gasped audibly and said, "What! You talked to the FBI?" "That's what I am here telling you," I replied quietly.

"You know that is against Party policy," she told me angrily.

"Listen," I countered, getting a bit hot myself, "if you'll recall, I haven't been in the Party for over two years. So I don't feel particularly bound by their policy."

Well, I went home again. I didn't tell George what I'd done. He didn't take kindly to having his advice ignored and I didn't blame him for that. It was 1952 and I forgot all about the whole thing for some time.

My boss called me in the next morning and admitted he had sent for the FBI because he wanted to keep me on the job. He said the FBI had reported to him that I "was not a Communist, but not an anti-Communist." I thought the diagnosis accurate. The boss said if I ever changed my mind I should be sure to let him know. Uh-hunh!

Anyhow, my appointment was made "permanent." My first step was to join the Credit Union . . . and the first thing you do there is to borrow $100 (or at least, that's what you borrowed in 1952). It was paid back by payroll deduction. Once it was all paid, you became eligible for a sizeable Credit Union loan. They lent money for anything except buying a home.

I worked on, studiously making myself as indispensable as possible to my Boss, Ed. We became fairly good friends. I recall no political discussions, just amiable chit-chat. He was a man who liked to appear "late for work." Starting time, 8:30 a. m.; he shows up at 8:50. I always arrived early, because I used the typewriter to do my correspondence and other writings. One of the checkers (we applied standards to workers' time sheets in order to calculate their bonus amounts) used to start at 7:30 because she worked in the "Stereo" Department, which started at that time.

I developed forms for keeping track of bonus payments and tied them into the daily time sheets. I began writing the quarterly reports for the Boss, based on interpreting the data in those sheets. And I was having fun, because he rarely pulled on the reins. He was having his own ball, frying those other fish.

About mid-way into 1954, I was sitting in the Boss's office with him. He had the door locked. We were looking at some highly confidential papers: the Company was hiring psychiatrists to evaluate the "leadership potential" of their young lions: who was "leadership material," who wasn't. Naturally, he had no business showing that manure to me. But whatever had to be done with the info was probably tedious from his viewpoint, so he was in process of turning it over to me.

Suddenly, the phone rings. Ed picks it up and listens for a second. I hear him say, "Well, hang onto to those papers; don't let them go any farther. And I'll be right up." He hung up and looked at me.

"Someone is circulating copies of the SAN FRANCISCO CHRONICLE around the building. It seems someone has fingered you at one of these hearings. You stay right here. Keep the door locked. Continue with what you're doing and don't let anyone in but me."

There were traveling circuses moving around the country in those McCarthyist days. They were called "Investigating Committees" and were usually headed by some Congressman or other more lowly Government official who thought he would advance his political career by persecuting the latest scapegoats (in this case, "Reds;" today, it's "Gays").

Their modus operandi was simple: they got their press notices; they settled in somewhere; they called in "witnesses," better known among the people as "finks." These finks would start naming local names. Those named usually joined the ranks of the unemployed in short order.

Now, it seemed, it was my turn. And who should turn up as the Bay Area fink but my former "prize student," Tim Evans, the self-styled carpenter. He told newsmen, "Everything I know about Communism and Negro History, I learned from Hodee Edwards." I was flattered. At the same time, I thought, had I been a black person, the last thing I'd want to confess was learning about the history of my own people from one of the enemy, so to speak.

I felt no resentment against Tim.

Obviously, he hadn't listened to my replies to his many (I now understood, inspired) questions. In my view, he was simply "betting on the wrong horse." If anything, I felt sorry for the poor boob. Didn't he even understand on which side his bread was buttered? Or, had he mistaken 30 pieces of silver for Money and a Future. Tsk!

Well, Karl Marx to the contrary notwithstanding, I got quite an education about the political savvy of the Great Proletariat during the week that followed this revelation about me. Delegations of workers who ran the machines, by definition proletarians, streamed to the Plant's Director, a kindly, mild-mannered gentleman named Eric Peters and demanded that they fire me. Mr. Peters' position was, "If she goes, they all go."

"Who, all?" I asked, when my Boss reported all this to me.

"Well," he drawled, "you're not the only Commie in this place, y'know."

"Zat so?" I answered. I knew of one other, but was rather pleased to learn that there were more. I thought that perhaps that explained a few vaguely familiar faces I had noticed around the plant when I went there on department errands.

"Yes," the Boss said, "Mr. Peters says the Company is not ready for this kind of publicity."

I supposed that was Good News.

As to my "fellow workers," to a person, their reaction was to start work precisely at 8:30 a.m. each morning. They did not look at me, or speak to me; I might as well not have been there. For years, I had told myself I didn't care what people thought about me. I still didn't, but if you've never been through anything like this, let me assure you, it's a damned weird feeling, not conducive to any kind of comfort whatever.

This went on for three days. On the 4th day, I was in at my usual early morning hour when who should I encounter but His Nibs, ole 8.50 a.m. starter, Ed. He breezed up to me and said, "You got anything to keep you busy this morning?" I looked at him but his poker face was on. "That's a helluva question to ask me," I said. "Well, start doing it and don't bother me." Hunh! I went to my office.

On the way, who else should I see, stumping toward me in her high heels but the checker from the Stereo Dept. She ignored me. She had left a news clipping on my desk the day before (she later admitted to this) showing a big apple, with some remark added on it about polishing. A sweet little expression of support and understanding, obviously.

I saw her go into Ed's office, followed by Ed, who closed the door. I could hear the lock turn. WHAT!? All morning, I noted a procession of department employees moving at intervals past my door. They all went into Ed's office and I could hear the door close and - a second or so later - the lock would click. I figured I'd hear about it in due course.

I heard about it sooner than I expected. First, one woman came to me and announced that she wished to apologize for her previous behavior. I assured her no apologies were needed. She said, "No, I promised Ed I would apologize, so I'm going to do it. I am apologizing because I condemned you without a hearing." "Well, thank you," I answered. "Your apology is accepted." There were several such instances. Finally, the checker from the Stereo Department came to me and asked me to step outside with her. 1 went along. The minute we were alone, she turned to me and burst into tears. Good God!

"I want to apologize for my behavior," she sobbed. "I don't know why I acted that way. It's not as if I never before saw a Communist. They haven't any horns."

"Forget it, kiddo," I said. "We all do what we have to do, it seems, so let's just put it behind us."

I wasn't being magnanimous; I just thought they'd possibly had their lesson.

Lunch came around. Then the procession into Ed's office stopped. It was about 2 p.m. I'd been saving some question till Ed's door was open, so now I took it in to him.

"Welllll," drawls he, "how are things going? Any better?"

I looked at this man. I had no illusions about his motives, but the fact that he'd dared to stand up and fight for his own position (he needed what I was doing for his department) convinced me that he truly did believe in "democracy." I was grateful. The situation had been very distressing.

"They've been apologizing all morning. D. burst into tears," I said, thinking I was conveying news.

"Oh, you should have seen it in here," he laughed. "Water was a foot deep, I swear . . . all over the floor."

That morning, before the 7:30 checker had come out of Ed's office, one of the male time checkers, Bill, had come to me in the presence of a couple of the others and had said, "Good morning, Hodee." I had nearly burst into tears myself. Then Bill had said he'd gone to see his Pastor the previous evening. Said he didn't feel good about what was going on in the plant over the revelations about my past.

The preacher had told him that because of the attorney General's "list" (of "subversive organizations," a list that was added to every few days as hysteria rose), anyone could be branded a "Communist" and that was why the Constitution had protective clauses in it like the Fifth Amendment and the First Amendment.

Things simmered down. Life and work went on.

I was driving an old Nash that looked sort of like an upside-down green bathtub on wheels. It was an "automatic," without the power to back up such a boast. Consequently, the thing couldn't get out of its own way, especially on a hill. George declared that stepping on the gas in that heap was like putting your foot into a bowl of mush. And now, things began to go wrong with it. Clearly, I needed a new car.

It was October of 1954. Ford distributors were putting brand new unsold 1954 models on sale at great savings. I went to the Credit Union. They agreed to finance a new car, but they wanted another $800 for down payment. I didn't have a red nickel. I asked, "How about a trade-in?" With straight faces, they accepted, and they also financed the down payment. It was paid by payroll deduction, the usual method at the plant. It took four years to pay for it, but meanwhile, I was driving it.

About a month or more after the above ruckus, who shows up in my doorway but an old friend, Annie. She said the Party had sent her to talk to me. I invited her in. I remember we were sitting on my bed. She hemmed and hawed around and then she said, "Uh, the Party understands that you talked to the FBI." That had been two years previous, but that thought did not occur to me until much later, for some reason.

"I reported that," I reminded her.

"Wellll," she went on, "Rudy (he was the California State Security Officer for the Party; watch-dog, sort of) was wondering if you would write some kind of statement for the Party about that. You know, like what you said, what they said, so on?"

I looked at the woman for a long few seconds.

"Listen, Ann, " I replied. "I already have a dossier in Washington, D. C. Now, if the Party wants to create one for me, too, they can damned well make it up themselves, cuz I am not going to lift a finger to help them with it. Is that clear?"

She shrank into her shoulders, smiled a rueful smile, and departed.

Next thing I knew, because someone told me (wish I could recall who), the Party had announced that Hodee Edwards was an FBI agent with whom there was to be "no association," their top punishment.

Believe it or not, it took years before I put together Tim Evans' antics, the CHRONICLE article about same, not getting fired over the revelations, and then starting to drive around in a brand new car. Perfect evidence, wot? Except they never bothered to ask me a single question outside of wondering if I'd do their bidding. There was no such thing as "benefit of the doubt." The shrewd political brains at HQ put 2 and 2 together and got a very simple 6. Pure genius!

Frankly, I now believe that this whole thing was a carefully worked out plot by the Feds in Party ranks which enabled the Feds to isolate me completely. See, I couldn't participate in "progressive" organizations because some slimy fink would whisper in an important ear that "a Red" was loose in their ranks; and I couldn't go near the radicals because the Party had officially knighted me an FBI agent. Brilliant!

As a result, I spent the next five years totally on my own. I brought up my kids as best I could. I continued to work at Moore Business Forms, Inc. Ed, helped by my activities, moved on to bigger and better pastures; Gus took over as Boss of the Department. Gus was one of the time checkers who took me out to lunch when The Incident finally concluded. Said he wanted to pick my brains so he could find out just how much democracy he really believed in. I think we are still friends.

I kept in touch with Ed over the years, but he literally destroyed himself. He used to confide in me about his "pecadillos," with women and booze. I knew his wife and she was a great person. He had twin girls and an unfortunate son who could not live up to his father's Great Expectations for him. Ed told me how Geoffrey had evaded the draft for our various Holy Wars, an evasion Ed deplored: the kid just went to bed and stayed there. He was killed in a factory accident some years later.

Ed died recently. In a convalescent home. He had had a stroke about ten years before up in Middletown, to which he had moved. The result of the stroke was to paralyze him from the chest down. He said he had thought he'd live fast and make a beautiful corpse. It didn't work out that way.

I stuck with him till I understood that he was using me against both of his daughters. His wife had long since left him. Sad end to a guy who was brave at least once in his life. I felt I owed him, up to a point.

Around 1957 or 1959, I decided I had had enough inactivity. The peace movement was gaining ground as we lost in Korea and then went into Vietnam. I could not remain on the sidelines any longer. So I went to the Quakers and told them I was a hot ex-Red but that I wanted to get going in the Peace Movement and wanted them to know about me in advance in case they had any objections. They said they weren't interested in anybody's politics as long as they acted for peace along with the rest of the organized peace lovers. Good enough.

Paul, Louee, and Steffen, 1958.

I marched in the first Women's Strike for Peace. I became acquainted with some superb women and felt good to be back in the mainstream again. In 1959, I was again visited by my friend Annie. She came creeping in and announced that she had come to apologize for her former visit and the role she had played in it. "You were just five years ahead of the rest of us," she explained. One by one, the old friends returned. I was so glad to see them all that I didn't care about the past.

My sons were growing up. My marriage to George continued to deteriorate. At one point, I had an affair with Dr. Holland Roberts of the American Russian Institute. In a way, it was my old friend, Margie, who laid the groundwork for that. Her husband, Jake; her father, Morris Keller, and George used to get together at each of our houses in turn on Saturday nights for some good pinochle. Marge and I used to go for ice cream and prepare the refreshments, meantime cementing our long-time friendship and catching up on each other's news for each week.

One of these times Marge said to me, "Honestly, Hodee, I can't understand how you can stay with someone who pays as little attention to you as George does."

Oh? I hadn't noticed. But now I began to notice. And when I was sent or went for some reason to the American Russian Institute or to the California Labor School (probably the latter), I ran into Holland. He needed volunteers for this or that, and I was a long-time habitual volunteer. Holland began to tell me how terrific I was.

Holland was always traveling the world as a delegate to various big peace conferences. His trips were always paid for by the peace organizations of the Left or by the Left itself. But this gave him prestige and there's nothing like "power" for making a hit with the ladies, I have found.

Climax of the affair came when I agreed to go away for a weekend with the courtly gentleman. I had not told George about the whole mess for some time; ashamed of it, I think. Afraid, a bit, too, I'm sure. But like all such things, it came out in the wash eventually. It was definitely not good for George's ego, a fact which I did not take into account . . . but then, he never took my ego into account when he was womanizing. I did tell him about the weekend and said that no matter what he said, I was going.

"Are you my wife or not?" he roared at me.

I looked at him. "As far as I am concerned, when I stopped loving you, I stopped being your wife," I flung at him. His mouth dropped open. It was apparently a totally new thought.

I went on the weekend. Holland had parked his car somewhere or other that he thought was a big secret. But I saw all the empty windows on first and second stories around and I could see shadowy figures moving. I knew he wasn't unobserved.

Furthermore, I had come to despise all the derring-do and subterfuge. If Marx were indeed correct, as I still believe he was for the most part, then what determines the course of History is not who has the best spies but something Marx called "The Relationship of Forces," meaning the relative strengths and abilities of the opposing classes involved.

Holland used to have a fit about some of my phone calls, made from his office on McAllister Street in San Francisco. "You should be careful about what you say on the phone," he told me once. "Why?" I asked. "What do I know or say that the FBI doesn't already know?" I added. He still thought caution was needed. I wasn't aware of knowing any "secrets," so I couldn't understand what he was on about. I gave him my version of "what decides the course of History," as above. He wasn't impressed.

Therefore, I wasn't surprised upon I returning from that weekend that I scarcely remember and found less than awe-inspiring, when George told me the FBI had called him not long after I had left. They asked him if he knew his wife was off with a famous Red leader or words to that effect. George said he was so angry over the whole mess that he was tempted to go along with the Boys, which was – as he realized – exactly what they were counting on. Instead, he declared, he told them he knew all about it and they should go to hell. I earnestly hope they did, but I doubt it.

If I needed any signs, this rather sad little affair was a sure one that my marriage with George was on the skids. Steffen, my older son, had gone into the Navy, where he distinguished himself until their "Intelligence" caught up with him, which took about two years (after which, they gave him a good grilling and a kind of plea bargain discharge). Paul, my younger son, became active in the Civil Rights Movement. He spent two months in somebody's jail for sitting in at the Sheraton Hotel in San Francisco in one of many attempts to force the hiring of minorities.

At one point, aware of our failing relationship, George and I took a trip to Los Angeles to see old friends who had moved down there. One of them, a plumber, was not to be found. He had gone, it turned out, to Ghana, where he was working for a Ghanaian plumbing company. "That's where you guys ought to be," said the friend who told us of Jerry's whereabouts. He gave us the address to write to.

Steffen and Paul, 1961. Photo by Harvey Richards

8. Moving to Ghana

George looked at me and I, at him. "I'm going," he said simply.

We got home and drew up a letter which we fired off to Jerry. In remarkably short order, a reply came back offering George a job in the same company as Jerry. He told me, "Listen, if an African country can make it to socialism, the world's got it made. Nkrumah says he is building socialism. Well, I'm going. I don't know what you're going to do. You can come along or not, as you please." He said Louee was going with him. She was 11 years old. It seemed to me it would be crazy not to go.

I resigned from MOORE BUSINESS FORMS, INC. It was December of 1960. We were by then living in a house we were hoping to buy. The job of disentangling ourselves from our possessions and roots was tedious, complicated, and debilitating. We asked the boys to come with us but by then they were attending college. They had their Dad, Harvey, who had long since married someone else and was living around Palo Alto, to turn to.

I sought out Mary Louise Hooper, a well-known Quaker woman from the Peace Movement, because she knew Ghana and Nkrumah. She said Ghana was now the "crossroads of Africa" and that every known tropical disease could be caught there, so she suggested I have every "shot" available. I did. I took 14 injections: typhus, typhoid, you name it, I had it. The last one was against yellow fever and it made me so ill I honestly thought I would die.

In fact, I became ill as preparations for the huge move progressed. My son Paul did all the packing; George did the rest besides helping with the packing. We lost the house; the woman who was to buy it never came through with the down payment that was to have paid for our trip and she kept, without paying for, all of our things she "bought" from us. There was no time left to seek another buyer for the property. In the end, we sent Marge and Jake the deed to the place from Ghana.

We set off for Ghana in at the end of 1961, destination London. Our first stop was in Canton, Ohio, with George's family. Then Boston at my younger sister Alice's place, where we spent two weeks. There, one of her children told Louee that I was not her real mother, a fact that came out in Sweden a month or so later. I spoke to many old friends and acquaintances by phone from there, including Nicolas Slonimsky from my childhood days at those Soirees. As far as I knew, we were moving to Ghana to live out life there, building socialism.

One important call George made from Alice's house: we phoned Ghana to get word on how to proceed to our prospective employment. Lou, the American involved in the company, told us come right on. We asked if we should get our visas in New York. He said, no; no need to do that; we could pick them up in London.

After Boston, the next stopover was New York to await departure on our SAS flight. We walked past the building in which the Ghanaian consulate was housed and thought of getting our visas while we were right there. But, no, hadn't Lou said it was OK to wait for London? So, alas and alack, we waited.

We traveled to London by way of Stockholm, where we spent a week, living in a cooperative housing development. Our host pulled a bed out of his kitchen wall, in which he slept, turning over his living room to us. You took your bath in a separate tub room.

It was here that Louee finally asked me point blank if she was adopted. Yes, I said, she was. She turned on her heel and from then on for a number of years spoke to me only when necessary. I was deeply hurt, having followed the book to the letter. I did not know what to say to make it easier for her - or myself, a state of silent hostility had set in to add to my troubles.

We had gone through Stockholm because the World Council of Peace was holding an international conference there and we were given entree by advance notice that we would attend. It was an exciting and enlightening experience.

Here, for the first time ever, we saw in action the growing schism between the Chinese and Soviet delegates. When we arrived, all the African delegates were standing around in the hall. They had walked out. George and I, seeing the plethora of committee meetings announced, decided to split up and attend different ones so we could compare notes.

The ones I attended really opened my eyes. To me, it appeared at first that the Chinese were "aggressors," that they were being "picky" and standing pat on what seemed like "semantics." I knew I was wrong when I attended one meeting and saw a Russian Bigwig come in and deliberately prevent a peaceful vote that had been about to be taken. He did it by provoking the Chinese to the point where they walked out and the meeting broke up. It was strong-arm tactics. Very disillusioning.

It was at this conference that we met Cheddi and Janet Jagan and we had fascinating talks. I later interviewed Cheddi and the interview was published in the San Francisco SUN REPORTER.

We reached London some time about the 8th of December in 1961. We found a "bed and breakfast" place to move into and, once unpacked, we had enough money to last us five days, by which time we were sure we would be in Ghana with George working.

The predicament we were in became apparent after what we thought would be a routine visit to the Ghanaian Embassy. We had left there the copy of the contract with "Tamakloe and Gardner" in Accra. We had signed it, but had to wait to arrive in Ghana for the company representatives to do so. When we returned to the Embassy to pick up our visas, the official who greeted us asked, with a puzzled expression on his face, "Could there be two George Edwardses?"

What? Then he showed us the reply from the Ghanaian Company. It read: "Job not ready. Can take no responsibility for your trip." The bottom had dropped out.

We had no idea what in the world had happened. We didn't know that George had been offered the job because someone named Troy who had had it before had walked out and left the Company short-handed. But on another visit to Los Angeles at some time before our departure, we had paid a visit to someone in whom George had confided our luck in his getting this job.

Nor could we know that whoever that person was, which I cannot now remember if I ever knew, was also a friend of Troy's and couldn't wait to tell him what had happened. We also did not learn till much later that Troy's reaction had been to fly straight back to Ghana and announce that he was back and since he was under contract, they had to give him back his job. The Company now had no authorization from Government to hire another foreigner. This occurred after we had talked to Lou Gardner from Boston and he had told us to wait to get visas in London.

Fortunately, Troy again didn't stay long in the job. Less than a month, I would hazard from the sequence of our events.

First of all, of course, our money ran out. Not before we had made a trans Atlantic call to my mother asking help. She had immediately wired us $300, a lot more money in 1961 than it is now. But American Express held onto that money for five horrible days, during each one of which they denied any knowledge of it.

We could no longer stay in the "bed and breakfast." During the stay we had run into some Americans in London. There were Grace and Dave and there were Lucy and Frank. Dave and Grace were very kind to us, lent us their apartment when they went on their regular Christmas pilgrimage to the Pacific or wherever by boat.. It was Frank and Lucy who saved our lives.

Frank was a Jamaican, teaching science in the London schools. Lucy was a pathologist, working at her profession somewhere in the City. They had just bought a house in a section of London to reach which George Eliot had had to travel by coach all day when she went on holiday in 13th century England. George's reaction to the end of our money was to suggest we turn in our tickets to Ghana and return to the States. Where to? I wondered. We'd burned all our bridges. To Ohio, he said. His mother and other members of his family lived there. I knew I'd never agree to that. While I adored his mother, I was not about to spend my old age in any Ohio.

I talked to Lucy and she said we were welcome to move in with them. However, they had spent all their money buying the house and had none left over for furniture, so the room was unfurnished. George said we would make them too uncomfortable if we moved in and slept on the floor so he was all for returning home. Not me.

I took matters into my own hands. George said we must not tell anyone of our plight. Well, I was sure, because all trans-Atlantic calls are monitored, that Someone knew of it in any case. I went down and found the landlady, who by then knew we were moving. I told her the whole miserable story, except that I could not then explain why the Ghanaian company had pulled the rug on us. I told her I had noticed a cot folded up in the bath room and wondered if she would let us use it. She said it belonged to the landlord but she'd phone him and see. He told her to give it to us.

Good! Now I had one bed. But we had no bedding. Grace and Dave were away on one of their vacations, but I managed somehow to find their landlady and told her our story. She was magnificent; she came up with bedding and another cot and all we had to do was to hire a cab or vehicle of some sort and get us over to Frank and Lucy's. We did that.

Just about then, a final call to American Express had revealed that they had the money for us. Somebody, I figure, got tired of waiting for us to turn up and beg for help to get home from the American Embassy. The thought did not even occur to me. I doubt that even having to face death itself would have let me entertain such a thought.

Joyfully I picked up the money. Of course, meantime, we were writing frantic letters to Ghana, sending radiograms and whatever, all without a response. Now, money in hand, we looked at a neighborhood bulletin board and discovered enough furniture to outfit the room for ten pounds, He got it and installed it and at least could leave that for Frank and Lucy when we left.

We waited, checking in with the Ghanaian Embassy daily. Frank and Lucy were totally wonderful to us Their two kids aroused all of us because of their British accents. Years later, in England, an Afro-American who was visiting me there was introduced to a young Trinidadian friend of mine who had gone to school in London with Louee. He, too, expressed surprise, "couldn't get over" Ann's pure English syllables. Amazing how stereotypes work!

Anyhow, one fine day, a telegram arrived at the Ghanaian Embassy saying, "Job now ready Proceed at once." What we later discovered was that Troy had again walked out and left the Company shorthanded. They could import one more foreigner.

The relief was incredible. George's reaction was, "Well, we waited for them. Now they can wait for us. We spent a week having ourselves a ball, going to theater, taking the kids to Covent Gardens to see the ballet (they put on Cinderella every Christmas, the way we do The Nutcracker), and so on.

In fact, I even decided to make a pilgrimage to Herne Hill, the last place from which I had heard from Havelock Ellis, and at least take a look at the house I had never visited, despite invitations from him.

I took Louee with me. I knew the old address, and after much wandering around in dense fog, we finally found it. I knocked on the door. A lady opened it. I could smell cabbage cooking somewhere inside. A bike leaned against a stairwell inside. I told her I was looking for the home of Havelock Ellis.

"Oh, he's dead, y'know," she screamed at me the way you do to people who speak a foreign language. I told her I knew that but was hoping to find out if she had heard of Francoise, or knew where she had moved to. The woman finally understood what I wanted.

"Oh," she said, "the foreign lady?" My heart leaped. I was onto the trail. Francoise had moved to another address in Dulwich. We kept walking till Louee was ready to drop. She was all for quitting and going home. Not I! I was so close, I couldn't possibly give up. We wandered about in the fog some more, given conflicting directions from each person we asked.

However, at last, we knocked on a door where the man said this was the wrong address, but the "foreign lady" had lived "over there across the street." He added, "But she's not there any more, y'know. She moved away somewhere to Birmingham or some such a while back." Well, since we'd come within smelling distance, I thought I'd knock on just one more door to see if anyone knew exactly where Francoise might be.

The first two doors made no reply; nobody home. At the third door, I struck gold. These people actually had, and gave me, her address. Delighted, I was able to withstand poor Louee's justified grumbles. We took a bus back and I wrote to Francoise. A letter came back, asking what I wanted with her. I replied, telling her who I was. My reward was an invitation to visit her.

I was unable to do that for lack of time at this moment. But later, on one of my trips from Ghana to England I did make it to Birmingham and met the charming lady, visited with her and was shown all the mementos of Havelock, given tea and cakes. It was

Old Home Week. I treasure the memory. Francoise told me that she and Havelock looked upon me as the the "dear daughter" they had never had. All her letters to me were also lost in Ghana.

Finally, on New Year's night, 1962, we found ourselves on a plane bound for Ghana, we were about to see one of the world's great continents; to live there, and hopefully become part of their life. Great vistas seemed to open before us.

The plane was air-conditioned. We had left London in the midst of sleet storms that whipped to the ground at a 45-degree angle and icy winds that cut through clothing with ease. I had on several layers with a cotton dress underneath, in anticipation of tropics. George wore his fedora and a warm overcoat.

The plane landed. It was an hour ahead of schedule. We prayed that someone would be there to meet us. The plane stood at its landing spot for a full 20 minutes, air-conditioning turned off, and all exits and windows closed. We began to suffocate. But even this came to an end. The plane door opened. Welcome to Africa. I stepped into the doorway. It was as if a hot wet towel had hit me in the face!

George stepped off wearing overcoat and fedora. It didn't take long before he began to peel out of them. Because we were so far ahead of schedule, it was another while before Lou Gardner, the American partner in Tamakloe & Gardner, turned up. He was a tall dark man with strange pale blue eyes, who rarely smiled.

In due course, we were seated in his open car driving along the main drag in Accra. Lilies of the Nile waved their blue greetings along islands in the middle of this modern street. Everywhere, women with huge bundles on their heads moved majestically along the sidewalk, clad in colorful cloth that fell to their feet. There was motion and excitement in the air.

"I'm in AFRICA," I kept shouting. Then, "Gee, it sure smells wonderful," I said.

"It smells, all right," was all Lou said. I thought it a strange remark at the time, but learned to understand it during my six years there, where open drains in the streets are commonplace.

George and I had set out for Africa with stars in our eyes. WE were not going to hobnob with the AMERICAN community. WE were going to become friends with the AFRICANS. We wanted to let "them" know that there were "good" Americans, the kind who understood and wanted to help, not plunder, Africa.

Noble, wonderful sentiments! The only trouble with them was that it took us two years - strange as it may sound - even to find, let alone integrate with, the African community. We found ourselves in the "European" sector.

George at work in Ghana, 1964

We began to learn how little we knew. For instance, it came as a shock to George to be greeted as a "European." The only "blacks" were Africans. No matter how dark the color of an American, he was still regarded - and rightly so, in Africa, I soon saw - as a "white man." Black Americans acted like Americans first; black men, second. The Ghanaians were polite and gentle and welcomed everyone with open arms. But they definitely knew white from black - and taught it to me, at least.

Our first home was on Labadie Road, en route to Nkrumah's [Christiansborg] castle. Traffic composed mostly of heavy trucks

Louee, George, Hodee and Diablo, the dog.
Kumasi, Ghana, c. 1962

rumbled by, supplying "Osagyefo" with food and whatever. It began about two in the morning, not too long after daytime traffic on that road had begun to quiet down.

When we first moved in, the electricity was not yet turned on. I opened the freezer compartment at the top of the big empty fridge standing there, and quickly slammed it shut. There was a - creature - in there; a mouse, I surmised from the size.

"Ooo, ooo," I squawked, "there's a mouse in the refrigerator."

Lou Gardner looked up from his conversation with George. He came over, opened the door and slammed it shut again.

"Mouse, hell!" he laughed. "That's just a cockroach."

Ohmigod! Well, here we were in Africa, sure enough. Nor did this aspect of that continent change as we remained there over the next six years. I met more than one of those indestructible critters, who have defied the so-called Law of Evolution by surviving

Louee in Kumasi, Ghana at home. c. 1963

unaltered for billions of years. With their bronze coloring and their buzzing flight that resembles the onslaught of a fleet of warplanes, they were just the tip of the iceberg in local wildlife, I soon discovered.

Take, for example, the black and yellow garden spider. A few of them used a three-day absence of ours from our Kumasi home to spin their webs over the back screen door. Even big George couldn't push it open: it took an axe. They seemed to live on the telephone wires, their long furry tentacles (I know they were legs, but who ever saw legs like that?) spraddled the parallel wires and the view you got of them was of a big round black circle decorated at its center with a neat yellow triangle.

This fecundity in vegetable and animal life prompted a wonderful Ghanaian quip: "If today you bury a dead horse, tomorrow morning you will have horse radish."

The heat in Ghana that helped to spawn such richness really got to me. The first five months we were there, I thought each, day had to be my last. At night, I could not bear even a sheet over me and slept with an electric fan at my feet blowing over my body. There was no question of closing windows.

Then, one day, we decided to take in another show at the Labadie Theater down the road. In Ghana, you go up to the ticket window, purchase your tickets, then go through the door into the "theater." The shock comes when you realize that all there is to the "theater" is a wall front. The audience sits, mercifully, right outdoors under the glorious, prolific, bright stars.

Audience participation is half the show: they cheer the hero, scream with delight when the kissing begins, boo and give violent advice to the villains. It was an exhilarating way to see a fifth-rate Hollywood movie.

On this particular evening, when we went into the theater and took our seats in the balcony, which was on the street level, I found that I had to pull my sweater closer around my shoulders against a breeze that arose. "My God," exclaimed George, "You've made it!"

Outside the bedroom window was a thatched roof propped up on four poles. This was a carpenter shop. Work continued, along with drumming and dancing and loud conversation in the African tongue, far into the night.

Another American we ran into was Libby Prussin, the only American working directly for the Ghana Government as an architect. She helped us through a lot of details and wised us up to plenty. She had a little Reilly car, a 1500, I remember it was. When she went on trek to the north, she occasionally left me her car to run around in. It was heavenly - even if not very frequent.

Louee went into a boarding school. Along with our other noble notions, we had decided that our child was not going to any American school; she would go to school with Ghanaians. It was a noble gesture; but alas, in truth the quality of education in the Ghanaian schools was not all that great and it was in the English, rather than the American, tradition.

However, that we found out later. She wore the little cotton uniforms and lived with Ghanaian girls in the dorms. She learned to recognize tarantulas and how to deal with them. She befriended several unfortunate dogs whom Ghanaians mistreated incredibly. She also treated me in a most distant manner, the overflow from her discovery in Sweden that I was not her "real" mother. Later, when we became friends, she told me she hated me for years. I'm glad I kept busy enough so that I didn't know that till she told me.

George's Company sent him "on trek" almost immediately. With Louee in school and George frequently away, I was, once again, totally isolated. I had nothing to do. Like a silly fool, I started writing to Holland Roberts again and George found out. One more link between us snapped.

Holland jumped at the bait and decided he was coming to visit me in Ghana. When he wrote that, I realized how idiotic I had been. The idea of having him actually arrive filled me with horror. I needn't have worried: he couldn't get a visa. I breathed a sigh of relief, but the further damage to my relationship with George was done: just one of a number of straws on that camel's back.

9. Journalist in Africa

One of the first things I did was to attend, on Feb. 5, 1962, a conference of Ghana, Guinea and Mali women. It was held on the roof of the Ambassador Hotel. The Harmattan, an annual wind that sweeps into West Africa from the desert to the north and cools things off notably in late January and early February, had begun to blow. The African women sat around shivering, wrapped in their great squares of colorful cloth. I could breathe again for the first time. There was AIR! "Hey, Obruni," they would say to me, seeing me sitting there with bare arms, "you like our Harmattan." I would agree fervently.

That conference was an eye-opener. I saw women there, two-thirds of whom spoke French, tackling problems common to all of them. No matter how long it took to gain agreement, there was never any wrangling. If an explanation was insufficient, patiently they began again. They kept at it till consensus was achieved. Never any shouting, gesturing, or signs whatever of anger or impatience. I was humbled by their largeness of soul and their political maturity.

On the first day, the Guinean and Malian women appeared in gorgeous diaphanous materials of pink, blue and yellow pastel draped artistically around the regular African women's wrap-around skirts and blouses. The next morning, damned if the Ghanaian women didn't turn up in the exact same clothing. They had sat up as late as necessary to imitate their "sisters," as the women referred to one another.

In this part of Africa at least, it is a sign, recognized everywhere, of "tight" friendship for two women to appear clad in identical costumes. That was what the Ghanaian women expressed, and what their French-speaking sisters understood, by their imitation of the guests' clothing.

I loved it - and I was learning, learning.

One day, I had an inspiration for a poem, which I wrote at white heat. I sent it to the Ghanaian TIMES, the main press in Ghana though not directly Government-run. On March 3, 1962, that poem appeared in print on the front page. Someone else brought it to my attention. I was launched as a journalist in my new country. After that, I wrote long letters of comment on all main events that we lived through in Ghana and almost all were printed. I joined the Ghana Press Club with credentials from the PEOPLE'S WORLD in San Francisco, as well as WOMEN OF THE WHOLE WORLD, in East Germany, where a few of my articles about life in Ghana appeared while I was in Ghana.

It wasn't long till George's running around was known to all but me, and it took a while before I found out. But in a way he did me a big favor. I am not one to sit and mope. I got out, got busy and made my mark in my chosen field. I was, at last and in deed, a real, a published writer.

As time went on, I got more and more integrated with their press, which in turn made me more and more involved in their struggles. Also, with these credentials, I attended every major conference held in Ghana, which I would then write up and send to various outlets, both in the U.S. and Europe, especially Eastern Europe. I appeared in London's PEACE NEWS, in San Francisco's SUN REPORTER, in the CHICAGO DEFENDER, in SOVIET WOMAN, and in almost all the Ghanaian newspapers.

My experience in Ghana was a crucial, pivotal time of my life. If I had not lived in Ghana, I would never have known what the world is really like. I did not live just on the surface; nor did I live within governmental or university shelter like most other foreigners. I met more and more middle level officials. I got along fine with them; they liked me. I loved them. I knew some of them were rascals, as their own people called them. But they were such charming rascals.

Moreover, I found I was able to speak intelligibly to those Ghanaians who could read English or hear it read to them. I developed influence among ordinary readers of the papers, as I discovered when I appeared at events run by various foreign embassies. Ghanaians would come up to me and repeat my latest quip, as when I characterized the two main candidates in the U. S. Johnson-Goldwater elections as "Tweedledee and Tweedledum," hardly the acme of originality. But Ghanaians just adore words and they rolled those around in their mouths and clapped me on the shoulder, smiling knowingly at me. I loved it. I loved them. It was just wonderful to talk to people and be heard.

And there is no doubt at all in my mind that my marriage to George and my years in the US Black community together with my understanding, however faulty or frail, of the theory of Marxism all tied to my daily contact with many Ghanaians, enabled me to see the situation in Ghana more clearly than most ex-patriates there, including the self-styled socialist people.

My advantage over Eastern Europeans, which of course they never did, nor would, admit (with the exception of Professor Rumantsev, my Romanian friend), was that I had had actual prolonged contact, living interchanges with black people. More, I had lived inside the capitalist system (that is, I was not dependent on Hollywood movies for my "knowledge" of "American life") and I had been brought up to "think freely," including about Marxism, which is not kosher with the self-styled Marxists.

Finally, long since disgusted with the impenetrable jargon in Marxist papers and journals, I forced myself to learn how to speak in plain English, or rather in plain language, which is not necessarily the same thing. Given the experience they were living through, Ghanaian ears were attuned to what I was saying, As they say, "they heard me."

Among the important international conferences I attended in Ghana during my stay were Nkrumah's "Conference of Third World Countries;" "The World without the Bomb," where I met

Julie Medlock; and the Conference on the Encyclopedia Africana, where I met, and learned to know a little, Dr. Alphaeus Hunton and his refreshing wife, Dorothy. In each of these events, I learned a great deal; in the last, I even played a positive role of my own, about which I hope to write in detail some day.

Once, thanks to a friend I made who was a travel agent in Kumasi where we were soon based, I was able to travel around on an official tour with real live Soviet Russians. From this tour, came a number of revelations. My seat companion on the tour was a Russian professor named something like Leo Preobrezhinski. He badgered and badgered until I agreed, against my better judgment, to tell him how I felt about the schism between the Soviet and Chinese Communists. He was not the least bit happy when I said I found the Chinese "correct."

Later, I found out he lied to the Huntons about what I had said to him. This I learned when I visited them at their home in Accra one time. They were upset when I laughed at the version this Russian, Leo, had given them of the incident in the bus. I told them what had really happened.

I don't know if they believed me or not, but it doesn't matter much, because I know what happened. It disturbed me no end that my Soviet "comrades" could lie about something so important, for motives still unclear to me. Maybe they'd heard the (officially circulated) rumors about my being "a CIA agent" and wanted their own "evidence" to condemn and isolate me from their precious colleagues. After my experience in Stockholm, I need not have been surprised.

I was able, during my stay, to get a close view of people from Eastern Europe, a view I cultivated assiduously: I had heard grumbles from some Ghanaians and I wanted to find out why.

The Russians were the worst, apparently devoid of humor and very very afraid of the loyalty of their own people, at least to judge by their actions, which even their "fraternal neighbors" deplored.

There was Professor Yanakiev, the Romanian professor mentioned above, who was present as a representative of the United Nations, not of his own land. I met Bulgarians; became friendly with a Polish couple and a Polish woman doctor, who I tutored in English. I developed a really good relationship with a Czech engineer who was teaching at Kumasi University and his North Korean wife who carried deep scars in one leg from shrapnel acquired during the American intervention there.

For a very short while, I worked for an American who was doing something or other for the Ghanaian Government representing the U.N. I quit that after two months because I thought I had run into a real CIA agent. First, my excellent instincts so advised me; but soon it was just watching him operate with Ghanaians. I figured I'd do Ghana more good by letting this guy do his own secretarial work than by helping him with it.

Not too long afterward, we were seconded, as they say, to Kumasi. Tamakloe & Gardner had some big jobs in and around this second city of Ghana and George was to oversee them. We were assigned one house by the side of the road. Later, we got another, much bigger, with a back yard, a papaya tree, a banana tree, a mango tree and hot pepper bushes (and I mean, HOT).

Eventually, I acquired a little German Prinz sports car with license SG12, in which I was able to run around in town, at least, and not be confined to that 48-foot living room, with no radio (TV was still unheard of, there) and no one to talk to.

At one point, Nkrumah's Government decided the time had come to educate Ghanaian students in the teachers' colleges about what socialism was. I was among those asked to prepare lectures on the subject. Since I had been writing articles along such lines, with the avowed aim of making the ideas comprehensible, I welcomed the opportunity to talk face to face with young Ghanaians on this, to me, exciting subject. Once the writing was finished, it was

The Sport Prinz

submitted to Accra for approval. Once approved, we were told it had to be delivered word for word as approved.

I gave one lecture. I also attended one given by an English socialist. I thought mine was at least interesting; his I found dull and full of the jargon I had come to hate. During the question period, I stood up to clarify some point he had brought up. I talked in idiomatic American. At the end of my short "explanation," the whole room burst into cheers, to my intense surprise - and satisfaction. I think the reason was that they were so relieved and happy to be able to understand what someone was saying to them.

But as soon as "someone" found out what was going on in Kumasi, word came down that the "so-cee-AH-leest" lectures were to stop forthwith. No sensible reason that I can recall was given. I strongly suspected the American Embassy or its agents. In any case, there I was again, with nothing to do and Louee at school, George always "on trek."

As I was walking to my car, I found Al Hadji Suleimana at my side, in his white burnoose. "Sulie," a long, tall skinny northerner with a sensitive pointed face and velvety dark skin, was from Tamale in Ghana's North and of Muslim faith. He was District

Secretary there of the Convention People's Party, the "ruling" party of Ghana with Osagyefo Dr. Kwame Nkrumah as its chief. There was very little of the rascal in Sulie, which other Ghanaians said was because he was a Muslim.

Sulie said to me, "Mama, I have a job for you." (All the Ghanaians, young or old, called me that. They said it was a "term of respect." Whenever I looked in the mirror, I earnestly hoped so.) This was welcome news.

"What kind of job?" I wondered.

"In the Fishing and Marketing Coop," he replied.

"But, Sulie," I exclaimed, "I don't know a thing about fish?"

"No, no, Mama," he replied urgently, "you will learn. It is very important. There is something going on. I want you to go there and you find out and report to me."

I had no idea what he was talking about. But I soon did, and the knowledge I gained there formed a whole addition to my growing political education.

The fish mongering women sold fresh fish to the citizens of Ghana out of the local markets. There was a notable protein lack in Ghanaian diets. There was no actual mass starvation there then, as in other countries, but I did see one case of this protein deficiency starvation, known as kwashiorkor: a child with a big belly standing out incongruously from a body that was mere skin and bones - and the face of an old woman. She moaned without cease. This was not for lack of food, but because of nutritional ignorance in so many rural areas.

Osagyefo was concerned about these unnecessary dietary deficiencies among his people. He devised a plan whereby the cooperatives run by the fishmongering women would have access to certain boats and whatever fish their crews caught, to be held in freezers at strategically placed centers throughout the countryside and sold to the people at 5 pesewas (100 pesewas made one cedi) a pound.

The project couldn't seem to get off the ground; nothing at all was happening. And then, strange stories began to come in to Party officials at local government seats. It was these stories that had upset Sulie and persuaded him to get me on their trail.

Because of the language barrier - I spoke no Twi or other African language, and these rural women spoke almost no English - it was not a simple matter to get the details of their story straight. I would come into the Coop Headquarters in Kumasi each day with my notebook and pens. The women would talk at length in Twi to Charles Essando Attu-Yedo, their official. In turn, Charles would translate what had been said. I would write it down as closely as I understood it. The next day, I'd come back and read what I had written.

They didn't want to hurt my feelings, so always they would say, "Yes, Mama, that is very good. But, you see, it was not quite like that." After a few days, I got used to this. The details were very involved, very convoluted, with various nefarious happpenstances intertwining with others. So, patiently, we worked, daily, for two months until one day, Charles said, "Yes, Mama. That is correct. You have got it."

What they disclosed to me reminded me of books I had read over the years exposing the corruption that had either tried to or had successfully overcome other, earlier, people's revolutions, as in the early Soviet Union, and in China.

At first, the Cooperatives had been unable to find a merchant with a freezer who would sell it to a Cooperative. When that barrier had been pierced, they ran into a new wrinkle: although Osagyefo had turned over to the Cooperatives two or three ships, the entire catch from each of which was to be for the Coops, the scenario didn't work out like that. They would send someone to Accra, where the fishing fleets came in, cold, hard cash in hand. They would ask for ten cartons of this fish, five of that.

Invariably, they reported, the reply was, "Ah, Comrades! SO sorry! We have only one carton . . . if you would like that?"

As a result, not only did the inland population not receive fresh fish to improve their diet; the price of fish for everyone in Ghana was maintained at a level which ensured the making of a number of wealthy men among certain "top level" Ghanaians.

I took my findings to the local CID, which was in the service of Nkrumah and the CPP. The gentleman I spoke to was flabbergasted, and visibly disturbed, by the information I brought him. He promised to investigate.

It was already too late. The fact that a situation like this could develop as far as it did was merely an indication of how badly the whole political situation had degenerated. By now, Nkrumah, pictured so erroneously as the Iron Dictator of Ghana who controlled all life in that country, was surrounded by graduate, if not teaching, rascals. He did not know what was going on in the country; all he "knew" was what his "advisers," the Rascals, told him. I wanted my report to get into the Old Man's hands. I knew there was no way that could be done by mail. So, I gave one copy to Tettegah, and another to Sulie. From each, I extracted a promise that he would not reveal the presence of the document to any of the advisors and would part with it only into Osagyefo's hands.

One of these copies made it, I learned after the coup from young friends, privy to "The Old Man," as they called him. In fact, one of them was there when the Old Man read it. He told me sorrowfully of seeing him explode when the truth hit him. My informant said he picked up a telephone and called someone. Angrily, he issued a command. The answer was, "Yes, Osagyefo, right away, Osagyefo." And that was it: nothing changed, except for the worse.

At the end of my work with the fishmongers, John Tettegah asked me to come to Accra again and work in the AATUF office there, writing for him as required. John was not only an official of the Ghana Trades Unions but also of the All-African Trades Union Federation (AATUF, known by its acronymn as Ah-toof), which had decided to open an office in Accra. I leaped at the offer.

Before I left, the Fishing and Marketing Coop gave me a farewell luncheon and presented me with a gorgeous hand-woven kente shawl that still hangs on my wall. They warned me to be careful in Accra because it was a wicked city. I told them not to worry, because the AATUF office was behind brick walls. Then, in no time flat, I was down there, living in the YWCA.

Some exposure of corruption in high places had begun earlier in the CPP's official organ, the EVENING NEWS. Its editor was Eric Heymann, one of the young hopefuls of the Convention People's Party. However, after a time, these exposures stopped.

I had made friends with a young man named Kwamina (meaning he was born on a Saturday). He wrote for various Ghanaian papers and was close to Nkrumah, who understood his honesty and treated him like a son. He and I had developed a very close friendship based on mutual respect.

There was an Afro-American woman named Esther who worked for the Ghana government, monitoring French radio. She lived in the "Y" in the room next to mine. We got to be fairly friendly. One evening she came home from her job and told me she heard on her French station that there had been an attempted coup in Ghana. Little prickles went skittering up and down my whole body. Frankly, I was not surprised.

I didn't know if she reported such things to the Government or to anyone and I didn't want to make a boo boo by asking. Instead, the next morning I jumped into little SG12 and high-tailed it to the Guinea Press. I was not allowed in, so I called Kwamina out.

When he arrived, I beckoned him to come close and told him what Esther had told me the night before. I said I didn't know if he already knew, but felt that I ought to tell someone and that was why I was here. He looked away from me and there was silence, so long it got awkward. He didn't say one word. I excused myself and drove away.

That evening, after I had gone to bed at the "Y", someone knocked on my door and said I had a visitor. It didn't take a moment for me to get to the lobby. There was Kwamina. He greeted me politely and asked if I would care to go for a cup of tea.

We got into his car and drove down to the seashore, where giant waves of the tropical African ocean beat the sand pugnaciously. For a few moments, we sat there in silence. I could sense that he was agitated and shaken.

"Mama," he began at last, "what you told me this morning, about the attempted coup here in Ghana, has been confirmed. It has failed, but I am feeling extremely depressed and at a loss what to do."

I said there was only one thing to do: that was to arouse the ordinary people and expose all the rascals, but at top speed. This was a few months before the actual end.

Osagyefo had promised Kwamina his own paper. This, after Kwamina had gone to him when the EVENING NEWS had backed off the exposures. Kwamina said he had told "The Old Man' that, if he would give him his own paper, he would not fear to expose to the last fact. That had been in February of 1965.

I had started work at AATUF and was there during all these incidents. I had been moved from a front to a back office at AATUF after some French African trades unionists arrived and saw me working there. They had stormed into Tettegah, asking, "What is that white woman doing in an office in this organization?" Tettegah assured them he would "take care of it," which he did with a shame-faced explanation to me as he settled me into a less visible place.

The change did not disturb my work. I wrote whatever was asked of me. Sometimes, it was an article "refuting" some slander in some foreign publication. Once, I was asked for and delivered an entire Chapter for one of Nkrumah's books, "Colonialism, the Last Stage of Imperialism."

Mine was Chapter 18 and it was reported to me that on receiving and reading my Chapter, Nkrumah had waved it in the faces of his assembled other writers and asked, "Now why can't you people write like this?" It appeared in the book verbatim, including a misspelling of the name of the current dictator of South Korea.

Also, after the book came out, Tettegah paid me a visit one morning. Said he, "Mama, the American Embassy does not like our Chapter 18 in Osagyefo's book." I smiled at him. "Good, John," I said heartily, "then we know we're right, isn't it?" His head jerked up and he stared at me as that reply sank in. "Unh," was all he said and turned and went off again.

I was in that back office one day in November of 1965 when Kwamina appeared and told me that Osagyefo had at last given him his paper. It was to be called THE SUNDAY PUNCH, and would run a trial issue in December. Kwamina asked me if I still wanted to work with him on it. "Try and keep me away," was my reply.

In practice, because of the controversy surrounding me in Ghana, especially my label as a "CIA Agent," my writings had to appear in the PUNCH without a by-line. That didn't bother me; I was feeling heavy, terrible political pressures and wanted to do all in my power to help my friends to stem the advancing tide.

What I saw in the seven weeks that paper lasted until the coup (and I have always believed that the appearance of the PUNCH and the reaction to it of the Ghanaians who found out about it became a factor which determined the timing of that coup) convinced me that, had Osagyefo not waited those ten months to fulfill his promise to Kwamina, there need not have been a coup.

From the first, the Guinea Press, the organization which ran the newspapers published under its aegis, "neglected" to distribute this crucial publication. I suggested to Kwamina that he should set up readers clubs all over Ghana and have them distribute the paper. "But Mama," he expostulated, "why should I do that? We have the Guinea Press distribution apparatus." "Yes, you do," I told him, "and do you see them distributing your paper?" He looked at me sort of strangely, because he knew as well as I that bundles of this paper had been stranded in railroad stations to all destinations out of Accra every single week it was published.

The response of the people who did know of the PUNCH and its deepening revelations of Higher-Up corruption was to send delegations to the paper, documents in hand. From everywhere these ordinary people of Ghana, the majority women, came and sat in the paper's narrow editorial office, a miserly space which should have warned Kwamina of the actual value officially set by his paper and the job it was to do. From factories and farms they came, exposing corrupt officials. As fast as he could get to it, Kwamina was printing the stories.

One day, Kwamina greeted me, saying, "Mama, now we have set up our first Reader's Club." It was somewhere by Takoradi, the big Naval installation of Ghana. "Good," I told Kwamina, "but let's get a lot of others, soon!" The winds of evil seemed almost palpable to me by then.

I did a series on "The Market Women of Ghana," because H. M. Basner, the white South African socialist, had written a column in the TIMES strongly suggesting that these women were enemies of the revolution because they were petty traders. After the first two of my series appeared in the PUNCH, Basner showed up when I was not there (for which Kwamina said he was thankful...I was contraband) and said, "You have some very good research people." Kwamina agreed that the PUNCH did OK. Basner tried to find out who it was, but Kwamina was non-committal. The last of these articles was due for publication the next day. On the eve of that day, an incident occurred: two of the young fellows who worked on the PUNCH for and with Kwamina were at the office. Kwamina called them to his desk. I was sitting opposite Kwamina; we'd been talking. Kwamina started to berate the two young men for having balked at some assignment on grounds that, "It's not my work."

I got up and started to leave.

"No, no, Mama," Kwamina said, "I want you to hear this."

I sat back down.

The guys stood there, heads bowed in shame. When Kwamina had finished telling them how he felt about this "colonialist" attitude, he turned to me and asked me if I wanted to say anything. I did.

"Listen," I begged. "Don't you guys know what is happening in this county? Don't you understand that great forces are actively working to take your country back from you? Can't you feel the evil around you? Don't you see there is so little time? We haven't got TIME," I was getting excited, but nobody stopped me, "to fool around with whose work is which. We must ALL pitch in NOW or nobody is going to work, do you think "they" will be kind to those of you who are exposing the corruption that enables them to take back your country?"

Kwamina looked at me with a tight smile and told the fellows to take heed and get on with it. My fourth story about the Market Women was typed up on newsprint, ready for typesetting the next morning. It was the conclusion of the series and I was proud of it and could hardly wait to see it. Tough luck, Rosie.

The next morning was February 28, 1966. I was in SG12 on my way downtown to the bank. 1 had arranged to fly to Tamale to meet George for a day or two, so was going to withdraw a few shekels for a plane ticket. We did see each other now and then, for I fear I still hoped that he would see the light, or me, or whatever and my personal nightmare would be magically gone.

There was almost no traffic. I thought that strange at 3 o'clock on a weekday morning. Maybe my clock was wrong?

Near the bank, I found a parking place and got out of my car. I started walking. Around the traffic circle there, I saw groups of people, lots of them, just standing around in twos and threes. I went and stood near some of them. There were murmurs, but mostly in one or another of the Ghanaian languages, but none of the usual loud cheerful cross conversations you could expect from such a crowd.

On the other side of the circle, half-hidden behind the usual shrubbery that decorated traffic circles, I could see a soldier in forest green fatigues and a green beret. He had a gun. Near him was a large forest green truck.

I kept looking around. Nobody greeted me. What the hell was going on? I couldn't stand the suspense another minute. So I went up to someone and asked.

"Don't you have a radiogram," he wanted to know. No, I didn't.

Everyone around started to laugh.

"The Army has taken over Ghana," were his next words.

"Pardon?" I couldn't have heard right.

But I had. I had known it the evening before at the PUNCH, but somehow, I still thought it would be next week or next month. I hadn't intended to be that accurate about the closeness of - whatever it was I had known was about to happen.

"Oh, my goodness!" I finally brought out. "I'm out of a job."

I asked what had happened to John Tettegah. "He's inside," was the reply. All important officials of the CPP were "inside."

The pretext for the coup had been the obvious and blatant corruption in Government. But its intent was to show in its deeds, especially its destruction of all the still small progress Nkrumah had achieved in advancing education, nutrition and other "social" assistance for his people. Free textbooks were abolished; free tuition was gone. Gone, the Nutrition Board and its trips to teach country women how to feed their children properly. These were all termed "frills." It was back to Square One – and I knew it was also the beginning of the end of my stay there. There would be no room for me, "CIA Agent" or not.

I went first to the North Korean Embassy. I liked those blunt, honest kind people. But I should have known better. I asked advice on "what to do" from the official translator, whom Louee had christened "Old Iron Hands" because of his hearty handshake. He looked at me benignly and said, "Go back to your husband." My heart dropped. But when I thought about it, what else was there for me to do?

I went back to Kumasi. SG12 gave up the ghost half-way there and I traveled the rest of the route in a "Mammy truck", along with Ghanaians who regarded my presence with some amusement. White people as a rule did not travel by Mammy wagon. This, of course, was not an "as a rule" day.

In due course, Kwamina showed up at my home and stayed with me for a month. I thought it not such a safe place for him to hide out, but I was glad of his presence and we talked at length about what had happened. One of the things he kept harping on was how wrong it had been to leave the distribution of goods in the hands of the expatriates.

I also discovered that, in the first panic of the coup, he had burned all the books I had lent him at his request out of my own store of them. Some were out of print and irreplaceable. I couldn't truly blame him. Who knew what the new "Government" which Kwamina assured me was "directed" by an American AID official would do?

It took a while for me to get out of the country.

Before I could do so, I received a summons from the Immigration Department. They said they wanted to "talk to me," They sent a Russian Volga auto to pick me up and take me to wherever it was they talked to me. I had wondered what they wanted. It didn't take too long to figure out.

They started their session by asking me if I had been out of Ghana since the coup. They knew I hadn't but I replied. They asked a number of questions, but that one cropped up twice. Finally, came one query which they tried to make appear nonchalant: had I been paid for my writings in Ghana?

THEN I understood what they were after. The "new" government had made much of the fact that the CPP had given Geoffrey Bing, a friend of Nkrumah's and of Nkrumah's Ghana, some 10,000 British pounds to set up a magazine about Africa in London, not a really munificent sum for such a venture by usual standards. However, on the strength of this "revelation," Bing and other English and foreign journalists who had also been "paid," oh shock and horrors! were "bundled out" of Ghana. That is, they were deported, by plane.

So, when the Immigration Department asked me if I had been paid for my articles, I was relieved and couldn't help playing my part to the hilt. Naturally, I hated to disappoint them but I did it in style.

"Oh, yes," I replied enthusiastically. "I was paid and it was because Osagyefo insisted."

Silence.

"Don't you want to know how much?" I asked because I couldn't wait for them to ask. They said, yes, they wanted to know.

"Forty pounds and five shillings," I announced in a triumphant voice. I could almost see the balloon collapse. In a few moments, they indicated that the "interview" was over and they drove me home through the rainy season muck in the lumbering Russian Volga. The irony of that tickled me, too.

All this time, I knew that my departure was fast approaching. But I had no idea what Louee and I were to do. The original plan was to go to England, stop over there a week or so, meet Richard Gibson and his family and then on back to the United States.

By now, I had been in correspondence with Richard for some time. I had first seen his name as Editor of the edition of a magazine called, "REVOLUTION, Africa, Latin America, Asia," at a Conference in Ghana. During intermissions it was customary for delegates to such conferences to meet until the intermissions were over.

At this particular conference, on the contrary, the delegates appeared to have found all available seats and were engrossed in reading a Readers' Digest type magazine.

After a few moments, I had to know what could be so fascinating as to prevent the usual talk fest. So I asked the dignified man in the burnoose next to me what he was reading. He passed the magazine to me.

I had never seen the publication before. I looked into the masthead portion and saw that Richard Gibson was the editor of the English edition. I took out his name and the Paris address of the magazine. At home, I had at once written to Richard and asked for a sample copy. He sent it. I read it. It was fascinating, non-stereotyped stuff about black life the world over.

I chose to write a critique of an article by James Boggs, the Detroit auto worker who was trying to set up protocol for his people in their struggles in the U.S. I finished it and fired it off to the Paris address.

Richard wrote back, saying he had liked my article and asking how I would like to contribute to the magazine.

I was overjoyed. I promptly sent him an article I had written about "The Role of Color on the African Political Scene."

Weeks went by and finally, hearing nothing, I wrote to Richard and asked if he had received the article. No reply. Kwamina had told me that seven countries (meaning Interpol) were reading all my outgoing and incoming mail in Ghana. That knowledge made me happy knowing that I wrote such long, detailed, political and analytical articles. Good enough for them, I thought, and I hoped they learned something, though 1 knew better. They already knew it all.

At first I feared that I had written something offensive in the article I had sent to Richard. But I also knew of the intrigues and counter-intrigues that went on in Ghana. So I began to think that maybe my mail wasn't getting through to Richard. I sent a copy of my letter off again, adding another copy to a friend in England asking her to mail it to France. In a week or so, I received a letter from Richard that was a shock and eye-opener.

In it, he told me how, earlier in his stay in Paris, he had been set up by an American "friend" of his whom he had known in school and in the American political movement. Richard had been a big factor in the success of the Fair Play for Cuba Committee set up to contain the Bay of Pigs madness, apparently successfully.

When the hounds got on his trail over that, Richard had said since the Committee was not a membership organization, there were no lists of members to turn over to anyone. And thereafter, he left the country, for good. He and I are still friends. He lives in England and expresses horror at the thought of ever returning here to live.

Later, I remembered thinking what a clever way he had chosen to thwart the Feds. I had not connected his name to that of the editor of the magazine I read in Ghana. In fact, it was some time before I put two and two together.

The letter he sent me told in graphic detail the story of this scam directed against him by the long-time "friend." The incident had taken place during the French war against Algeria. The political scene in Paris had been messy enough at the time. But this frame up now came up again because Jacques Verges, the editor of the main French edition of the magazine, owed Richard, then married to an English Jewish woman and father of two small children, ten months' wages and Richard had begun getting a bit impatient about receiving what was due him. Verges had gotten out of paying Richard by the simple device of resurrecting the old frame up. Thereby, he also had Richards labeled as - you guessed it! - a CIA agent.

The net effect of this ploy was to remove Richard as editor of the very successful, intensely interesting to Africans, edition of the revolutionary magazine I had first seen at that Accra Conference and from which had stemmed Richard's and my life-long friendship. That developed after he found that I did not fall for accusations. Richard had expected me to join "all the others" in spurning and denouncing him. I don't denounce on anybody's say-so, especially when that say-so sounds suspiciously like something bad that had happened to me, also on "say-so."

To me, Richard's story rang true, and having been through my own version of it, I believed it. Being what I am, I decided to DO something about it. On my next trip to Accra, I tried.

I went to see the editor of THE SPARK, the theoretical paper of the CPP. I showed Kofi, its editor, the letter. He told me he believed it and that he was going to Paris that week and would talk to Richard. I gave him Richard's address and wrote Richard an obscure letter about "expecting someone to visit him." I believe Kofi mentioned his intention to someone before leaving and was told under no circumstances to visit Richard, so Richard never received any unknown visitor.

Next, I had written letters to people all over the world. That included one of the Editors of the MONTHLY REVIEW. The story about my own and Richard's alleged "connections" had obviously preceded my letters. The only one who responded favorably was a guy named Lionel, then in Indonesia, whose name Richard had sent me. And Lionel did try to help Richard for a while, but he ended up rifling Richard's file drawers later (at whose behest, I wondered?) when Richard was sheltering him at no cost in his own home. Lionel added up to a big disappointment.

However, my very first stop, in my innocence, had been to Shirley Graham Du Bois. To my surprise, she threatened me with deportation from Ghana (she had Osagyefo's ear, thanks to the prestige of her late husband, the great scholar and historian, W.E.B. DuBois, whom we met in Ghana before his death) if I didn't stop agitating about this matter.

Later, I became sure that this incident helped Shirley to play an unsuspecting role against me, and, under the circumstances, speaking without false modesty, against Ghana's real interest.

For, at one time near the end of Nkrumah's regime, as the CPP's official paper, THE EVENING NEWS, began to expose corruption in Government (till the trail led it "too high" in official ranks, when it backed off), I was summoned to Accra by Eric and told a number of flattering things about my writing, and Osagyefo's regard for them. It seems that Osagyefo had asked Eric whether or not I was being paid for my writings. When Eric admitted that I was not, The Old Man had suggested, Eric said, that I should be. In fact, he went on, there was a job for me on the NEWS.

And, he added, it was not impossible that I might actually meet Nkrumah in person. That one, I privately did not believe.

However, on the strength of these encouraging words, I hung around in Accra, living at the "Y", still working at AATUF, hopefully awaiting my summons from Eric. After some time, when it had not arrived, I went to see him. "Ah," he told me, "we are waiting to get a house for you." I could feel myself swelling up inside with impatience. I assured him, I didn't want a house and that I would be perfectly happy with an apartment just so I could sleep, cook and write in it.

More time went by. Again I sought Eric out. This time, he hemmed and hawed and said that "some of the comrades" felt it would be "awkward" to see a white woman on the staff. I countered that I didn't need to work AT the paper; I could easily work out of my room. All I wanted was to be allowed to start making my contribution to Ghana and to Osagyefo's programs.

At the end of a much shorter wait, I was suddenly summoned to a meeting at the EVENING NEW'S Headquarters. It seemed there was a new journalistic advisor. We all cooled our heels till he appeared, which I understood emphasized his rank and importance.

He turned out to be a Ghanaian who had been graduated in Journalism from an East German University. I got the impression that he was the one who had put his foot down against hiring me. This, because Eric told me Osagyefo's reaction to the whispers against me was that, for his people, he would work with the devil.

So someone with transferred Higher Authority must have advised him against such a course.

After this new Eastern-European-trained journalist's belated arrival, Eric began to speak. He didn't actually hem and haw, but the speech was a hem-haw in itself. What he said was, they were all uneasy because "Osagyefo had been told on good authority" that we might have a CIA agent in our midst. I heard the knell for my career as a journalist in Ghana. My brain was scrambling like a squirrel in a cage, but I played it cool.

I told them about the high-level Czarist agent who had wormed his way into the Central Committee of the Russian Communist Party before the revolution there. I said that, when he was discovered, Lenin had noted that it was not a totally negative finding, because – to get to such a high Party position – the worm had had to do some good things for the revolution.

But, I now added, if you think someone is a CIA Agent, you not only refuse to give that person a job on your official paper; you do not publish their theoretical writings or their by-line to give them prestige.

And so it came about that, for the last few months before the coup, nothing by H. W. Edwards appeared in any newspaper or journal published in Ghana. I returned to Kumasi, to the empty house and began to work on a book. After the coup, there was absolutely nothing for me to do, so I spent all my time studying and then writing - and rewriting.

After that meeting, the next time I saw Kwamina, I tried to pry out of him who could have told Osagyefo that I was a CIA Agent. All he would says was "someone" in a high position.

I had been sure for quite a while that there was at least one real CIA agent in Ghana with an indirect or perhaps direct path to the Chief of State. Kwamina's reply didn't help me to any ideas about the person's identity. But, since I already knew the truth about myself, what this incident did was to disclose to me the existence of a real agent. In fact, I told Eric, "Find out who told Nkrumah that, and you'll have a real CIA Agent." And I couldn't then penetrate the meaning of Eric's odd little smile.

But after the coup I understood, when Kwamina finally told me that the "someone who told Nkrumeh" had been none other than W.E.B. DuBois' widow, the well-meaning Shirley Graham DuBois. And once I knew that, I knew who the Agent was. I knew it couldn't possibly be Shirley; she didn't have the astute political sense of her late husband.

I also knew, however, that she herself had imported one person into Ghana, installing him as Head of Ghana's School of Journalism. HE was none other than the one whom Richard had named to me in his letter as having "framed" him in Paris in days not too long past. Later, in England, Richard told me of the close ties from USA days between Shirley and this man. That completed the picture. Kwamina had not known about this person, because I'd never told him the story. During his stay with me after the coup, we put our bits of story together, for all the good that did.

During my hibernation in Kumasi prior to finally leaving, I dug up and restudied Lenin's two classics "The State and Revolution" and "Imperialism, The Highest Stage of Capitalism."

My! How differently their message read now that I had lived through some real live politics! They no longer appeared as "theory," but as practical guides for how to act in situations like the one I found myself in. I also got out a book of Lenin's entitled, "Against Revisionism," meaning the revision of "true" Marxism, and I studied it till the pages nearly wore off. It took me eight years to write that book, and its sequel.

I had not been hurt or damaged by the incident at the EVENING NEWS, but it had been one sign of the net tightening around this country which I felt its own people, especially those supposedly "knowledgeable," were totally over-looking.

Because they themselves were so kind and generous, they did not understand the ferociousness of The Enemy. They did not realized what an incredible financial stake a colony, real or "neo", represented to its "investors overseas." But that was what I learned out of this and all the rest that happened to me, both before and after my sojourn in Ghana. It was that knowledge that made me write my books when the coup deprived me of any other useful occupation.

In the middle of all this political turmoil, Louee and I had established that "Papa" as the Ghanaians called George, had a girl-friend in Tamale. We had seen them park at the Rest House in that city. I knew I had another, urgent, personal reason now to get out.

At first, I had begged George to get me a plane ticket from the Company, which was bound by contract to pay the fare home for any expatriate employee or his family.

But time went by and George didn't lift a finger. Finally, I went to Accra myself and spoke to "J.K." as Tamakloe was known. By the end of the day, I had my plane reservation. I'd given Louee a choice to remain with her Dad or leave with me. To my pleased surprise she chose me. I had contracted malaria and dengue fever at different times and during one of these times, Louee told me she had seen George with some woman in his car when I was lying at home in bed. This had outraged her and so now she opted to leave with me.

10. London

As a result of my open support for Richard when the entire world was denouncing him with no proof whatsoever, when Louee and I were ready to leave Ghana, Richard and Sarah, his wife, said they had room to put us up in their new home for as long as we needed. We had a destination as well as a point of departure.

Richard met us at the airport and had no trouble identifying us though we'd never met in person. George, however, deserted us. Though he "promised" to send us 50 English pounds a month, nothing, not a farthing, ever came. I'm sure he has his usual innocent explanation, which always manages to make me the untrustful villain of the piece.

Louee in London, 1967

This turned out to be the start, for me, of six years in England. Louee started to school almost immediately. She had quickly made a friend, a Trinidadian girl, Ann Clarke. Through Ann, I met her mother, Stella, a piano teacher and a thoughtful person. Stella had the delightful rollicking West Indian accent, but Ann spoke pure English. She had been in England from the age of three.

As a result, we did not leave England in a week, as planned. Instead, we decided that Louee should finish at least her high school education in the English system, now that we had spent six years in Ghana where the same system was the one under which she had studied for six years.

We stayed with Sarah and Richard and their three kids, now grown, for eight months. At first, I worried and worried about not being able to pay for our keep. Then, I began applying for jobs. Someone who lived in England and knew the ropes told me my Harvard degree would get me a teaching job. They also said that my AGE would be worth money, too. Right on both counts!

I taught in two schools. The first was a summer session, in a muggy July, at a working class school in Kent, to which I traveled by train each day. The ad I answered said I was to teach "creative writing" to these children and I had jumped for joy at being hired. Alas! The ad was a come-on.

What I did was substitute teaching, any subject, whether I knew anything about it or not. If I didn't, I took the kids out on the playing field and we spent the time sitting around. These kids had jobs waiting for them when they got out of school at the nearby airplane factory where their parents worked. So most of them were just passing the time till their fifteenth birthdays, the legal age for dropping out in England.

The second school was a "Church of England" School, St. Margarets, in some toney part of London, complete with lilacs and flower garden. However, since 75% of the student body happened to be Jewish, we were spared the weekly "religion" class and held, instead, a "Discussion Period."

While I was teaching there, a great demonstration against the Vietnam war took place at the American Embassy, located in Grosvenor Square. Naturally, I was there, one of a huge mob. So, I did not stand out. Yet, somehow, that night, what face should appear, however briefly, on English TV but...?

In Ghana, someone who I thought should know had told me that both in England and in Ghana, George and I were followed everywhere by the CID. I had a bit of evidence of that once or twice from incidents in England which I can't go into here. So it didn't surprise me to learn that my "fizz" had appeared on English TV.

At discussion class, the next day, the kids asked me if I had been at the demonstration. Obviously, they had seen the TV, but waited to see what I'd say. "Of course," I told them. "That's where any good American should have been yesterday."

One member of this class happened to be the daughter of an American Embassy employee. She complained bitterly about the demonstration, saying it forced her father to stay at the embassy for 48 hours, thus "depriving his family" of him. The English kids took her on, telling her it was a petty personal and stupid reason for objecting to the event. "In England," said one lassie, "everyone has a right to their political beliefs."

Not too long afterward, unable to solve a discipline problem in one of my classes, I walked out and went to the Teacher's Room. The girls came to apologize and assured me they DID want to learn and I should please come back.

Shortly thereafter, I had a flu-like health problem but nonetheless went on teaching. I was in the Teacher's Room when the Head Mistress came and scolded me in front of the other teachers about having left a class room. Being sick, I disgusted myself by bursting into tears.

I am dead certain that the father of that American student must have contacted this woman and told her "it was his daughter or that teacher." Well, his daughter was paying tuition; "that teacher" was drawing money OUT of the school. Since it is illegal to fire anyone for political activity in Jolly Ole England, she had a little problem on her hands.

My little hike out of that class room gave her the hook she needed. She sent me a letter suggesting I find some other occupation than teaching – for which, she assured me in writing, I was "not suited."

Hodee in London

That came as a surprise: in the Teacher's Room one of the British teachers of English who had seen the work of one of my classes, had asked me how the devil I got the kids to do such marvelous work. I don't know now and I didn't know then. I guess it was because, never having taught before, I didn't know what to expect, so expected – and got - the best.

Anyhow, I was out of work again. I went to work as a "temp" for a few weeks. And then one day I answered an ad for a "secretary" for the Institution of Mechanical Engineers. Oh, Boy! That was for me! I was eager to get in there.

However, when I went for my interview, I was told that if I didn't take shorthand at 120 words per minute I could not get a secretarial position in England. This was a bad disappointment. After all, I had an academic background in Physics, didn't I?

Just as I was about to shuffle out of there, totally dejected, I happened to remember having with me a little document I had sent off to my friend and ex-boss, Gus, at Moore Business Forms: a "testimonial." Someone had suggested that move, assuring me that the English set great store by testimonials. He had written me me a humdinger; in fact, when I read it I sort of wondered who in Hades he was talking about.

Now, I pulled this out and let Peter Davies, the Englishman who was interviewing me, read it. He hired me. But not as a secretary. He admitted there was another job going, one to which he had not expected to hire a woman (let alone a foreigner, thought I) because "there would be no supervision, no one to tell you what to do."

The job was to build the sales of the Bound Conference Volumes published about 11 times a year by IMechE. It seems they were losing about 1,000 pounds a week on these publications because nobody knew they were available. He said a lot of people objected to "promoting" the sales of these (obviously sacred) tomes, but he thought it a practical idea. I just said, "Lead me to it!" And he did.

I had only just obtained the job, when I got a trans Atlantic call from Louee. She had gone home as an Camp Counselor and was calling for permission to stay in America. I would have joined her, but I had just obtained the job at IMecht and was most anxious to try my hand at it.

So Louee returned to "Little Golden America," while Mama did her thing in England.

For the next four years, I worked at this job and built the only exclusively, or mainly, industrial card index in England. It got to

Hodee on her 3 wheel moped, London.

be 60,000 strong and I had advanced to a decision of wanting to prune it when I left England and went back home.

I did a good job of it while I was there; traveled all over Great Britain to conferences to make book displays, an expense that was excised during my last year there, since we couldn't show any real sales improvement as a result (nor had I really expected them, but it was a marvelous way to see England without any money of your own).

The job at the IMechE became more useful to me and more interesting as I began to make friends among some of the employees. One person, for instance, made my life a lot easier by bending the rules about no one being allowed to have a key. With that key, and a three-wheeled moped I invested in, I used to show up at 5 a.m. at the solid British building, go up to my office on the top floor, and there, work on my book.

And working on my book began to involve me in the Left in England. I needed to get into the British Museum Library and any other storehouse of references, where I could piece out the scanty information that had been available to me for background in Ghana. Someone put me in touch with Malcolm Caldwell, a professor at London University and a world recognized authority on Southeast Asia.

Malcolm proved a real treasure. His Scottish accent made music in my ears, to begin with. He knocked himself out, helping me any way he could, and did get me into both the British Museum Library and the Political Library of London University. I became well acquainted with him.

He said he "believed in" my book and that it "must see the light in print." To look at him, you'd never guess he was a professor or a world-renowned authority on anything. He was a kind of a hippy type. A real mensch, as my mother would say. After I had returned to the U.S., when he was on tour in this country, he came by to visit me once or twice and I was anxiously awaiting his next visit when news came over the TV that he had been blown away in Cambodia, where he had gone to find out the truth about Pol Pot. I felt this a sad loss to the people of the world, whose real friend Malcolm had been.

I also became involved in a group called "The Finsbury Communists." I can't recall how or where I met Ivor and his rosy-cheeked, always cheerful wife, Flo, whom Ivor was always telling to "shut her face," while I thought her terse comments on whatever we were discussing were right on.

When I came into the Group, I was living in the Camden section of London and apparently, so were a number of other "cum-raids," as the English called each other in these groups. So we formed a kind of Branch of the Finsbury parent body, and called ourselves the Camden Marxist-Leninist Group.

Our main job was putting out a periodic newsletter. I liked the way they went about it. Before a newsletter went out, a subject, deemed to be timely, was assigned. Everyone went home and set forth their ideas on subject. A couple of weeks later, a discussion was held. Then one person was designated to write the consensus to be run as the newsletter. After I came there, I wrote a number of them. The only thing was, if any phrase, word, or idea appeared in such writings, that could not be accepted unanimously, it was simply cut out. Thus everything they

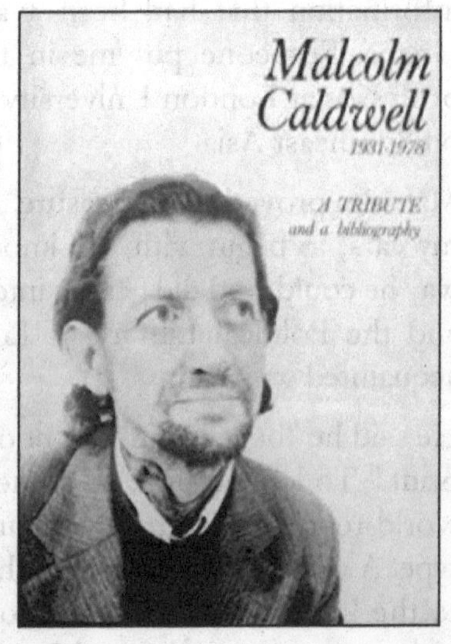

issued represented the unanimous opinion of those present. I think the most of us there ever were while I was there was five.

There were also a number of conferences that were held discussing the plight and possible solutions for the so called Third World. There were loads of such people living in England: refugees, people on their way somewhere who got stuck there, students, etc. I played an active role in at least one of these. In fact, that was where I first met Malcolm Caldwell in person. We were both scheduled speakers there.

My previous dealings with him had come about through an article he had printed on North Vietnam in a well known paper called PEACE NEWS, for which I also wrote, so that I knew the editor, Rod Prince. Malcolm repeated a number of what I considered slanders about the brave North Vietnamese Government so, as a patriotic American, I wrote a reply, politely lambasting Malcolm for daring to say such Stuff under the cloak of being an Authority on the subject.

The editor had objected to the nerve of this upstart American criticising a world-renowned Authority. As usual I stood my ground and Rod Prince and I became friends.

Later, Malcolm had made a trip to North Vietnam and had come home and written an article totally taking back his former slanders. I had admired his honesty, especially in view of his status.

When I had met Malcolm at the conference and gone up to make myself known to him, I'd been a bit worried about how he would receive me. I needn't have. He said, "Don't give it a second thought. You were right and I'm GLAD you wrote to PEACE NEWS and set the record straight. " What a tragedy for such a human being to have been murdered! I'm glad of the short time I did have to know him.

In such activities four years passed. My family was pressuring me to return home. "The grandchildren are growing up without you," they argued. Then, IMechE gave me a push: my boss said he was promoting me to be Head of Sales for the Publication Department with three people working under me.

I was delighted, but asked for a better wage. The man looked at me as if I'd gone cross eyed. When I noted that he'd never get a MAN to do the job for less than I was asking, he looked "That's right."

That did it. I went home, packed my Things and shipped them off to America to the West Coast. I had worked at IMechE for four years. After three years, in England, I had four weeks' paid vacation coming to me. However if I were to announce that I was quitting, I'd have lost all of it.

The year before, on vacation, I had got the IMechE to pay my fare over and back in exchange for investigating the reaction of various Universities and Institutions to a plan IMechE had to issue its own Automotive Journal ' in competition with that of the S.A.E., the Society of Automotive Engineers of the U.S. Everywhere, the reception was lukewarm. I was convinced by the end of my trip that they were throwing good money away to start the project and issued a report saying as much.

I had noticed that the gentleman heading the project, whose idea it had obviously been, considered my presence, whenever he happened to be conferring with my boss, at least unnecessary. The Boss had asked me to be present since I was going to look into the matter in the U.S. The other guy would wait patiently for me to shut up and then go on talking as if I hadn't said a word.

11. Back in the USA

After my return and reading my report, they ignored my advice and all the documentation I'd sent with it and launched the project. It lasted about two years and then folded, I never said, "I told you so," but that would have been a pleasure.

Thus, in July of 1973, I landed at San Francisco airport, home again after nearly 13 years abroad.

I arrived totally without identity. A passport won't get you credit worth a tinker's dam in this country: if you ain't got plastic, honey, you ain't nobody, with a big "N".

I had been invited to stay at my younger son's house. His wife had just had a new baby. I blew the whole scene. I was scared and penniless. My English vacation money and back pay owed me at the time I left should keep me afloat, but for how long? And what about when it was gone? As a result, I paid no attention to the problems Susie was having, lifted hardly a finger to give her a hand and in general I guess I made them sorry I had answered their pleas and come home.

In any case, I was told I would have to leave. I had no idea where I could go, but fortunately, someone needed a house-sitter for a couple of months. So I went and did that, and meantime, finally got a job at a department store. Hallelujah! The first thing they did was to issue me a credit card; as they do for all their employees. At last! I was Someone again.

I stayed there for ten months, working myself right out of a job. The guy said there was too much paper around the place and I should find out why and do something about it. I did. I worked up procedures that gradually made it unnecessary to have more than two employees. I was the third and I could see that, once I'd done my job, the Boss had no further need of me, was never going to find anything for me to do nor give me the raise he had promised when I first arrived. Besides, on that job, you had to punch a time clock going in and coming out. I resigned.

Next, I got a job in the catalog department of a place that sold scientific instruments. The job lasted two years, after which it became apparent that these jobs were really only part-time, since the catalog appeared only every second year. All the jobs were eliminated and temporary employees were hired (so that the Company need not pay "benefits").

It was while I was at this job, I suppose to prove that there was still a little life in the Old Girl yet, I began a nine-year, off-beat relationship with an old Teamster. I knew he was married; he knew

Hodee and Paul, Piedmont, CA 1973

I knew it when he made his interesting suggestion in 1976. Seeing that he knew, I blithely agreed, or at least, I said, "Why not?"

Donald really treated me better than either of my husbands, if I measure treatment in terms of demonstrated respect and both verbal and material expressions of appreciation.

Because of him, I joined the Organ Club to which he belonged. For a teamster, he sure has a fine-tuned musical ear and had taken lessons, starting at age 55 (he was 63 when I net him) till he plays very nicely. He is a master at creating interesting chords for the familiar melodies. In fact, he could (if he could ever overcome his lack of certainty about his own ability) make a really fine musician.

I even bought an organ myself, took lessons, and tried to learn to play. I also became an officer of the Club due course and during my two terms as President and my term as Program Coordinator, we had the liveliest and fastest growing such Club in the Northern California area.

The Club membership was mainly elderly and very conservative, though most of them had worked for a living to "get where they were." I have no doubt that my past followed me into Club ranks and jealousy at my success became stronger than the desire to have a good time. In nothing flat, they squeezed me out of leadership and ran the club into the ground.

I finally broke off my relationship with Donald in early December, 1985, because it just got sticky, due to his guilt feelings. Worse, it had become boring, beyond which nothing on earth can survive.

Back at the scientific instrument company, when the Catalog Department was turned into a temporary job, they helped me to move into another department, where the work was tedious and mind-numbing. After some months there, a job opened up in Customer Service. I applied and was hired by the supervisor of the time who had worked with me in the Catalog Department

Hodee as President of
the Organ Club.

before the permanent jobs had been abolished. He said I was just the person the Customer Service Department needed.

Everybody knew that but the Customer Service Department. On top of that, the guy who hired me evidently, was made a supervisor before he had been thoroughly trained; the job involved a lot of computer work and endless detail. So they demoted Chuck and put someone else in charge. He left the Company.

Then they switched the whole operation into the Credit Department on the basis that the reason people didn't pay bills was because of a customer service problem of some kind or other.

The head of the Credit Department was a Wise Guy who didn't know how to deal with any woman whom he couldn't address as "Chickie." I most obviously was no "Chickie. " He had a girlfriend, whom I think of as his Moll, whom he had made head of the new Customer Service operation. She had problems with her Mother, so I didn't look too good to her and she flat out refused (in action; promises were plentiful) to give me any training. Then she got sick of even looking at me and listening to me asking for the training, so she moved me out of her office into a hallway.

There ensued a period during which I fought not to be cut off from my job just before I would be eligible for a (small) pension that came with the job. I told Management that if they dared to fire me over this I was taking the case to the Equal Employmennt Opportunity Committee, EEOC. They knew I had a case, because I had received totally different treatment from a 19-year-old who had been hired for the same job. So, instead of firing me, they offered me a job in the Mail Room, sure (no doubt) that I'd refuse it. When I found out they couldn't touch my salary, I grabbed the job. There, I coasted to my 65th birthday and retired on pension on that birthday, Dec. 18, 1979.

In the end, there was a shake-up in the Credit Department. The Moll was taken out from under the Boss's jurisdiction and put under someone else's, a move which did not please her in the least. When the new supervisor dared to make a suggestion about her work, she told him that she knew all about Customer Service and to get off her back.

In April 1983, I went in with my younger son, Paul Richards, to try to help him build his own business as a Home Inspector. He had not enjoyed working as a construction worker, but his experience in that field had qualified him to do home inspections, We started from pretty close to the ground and built the business. It went through a number of vicissitudes, but he is now in his own Corporation and we are back in Oakland, after a four-month interim in San Francisco, trying to amalgamate with Paul's former

Boss, who had started him in the inspection business. This merger did not work out, and we had to start perilously close to the bottom again, but we did it. It was just after we gave up the attempted merger and the office-sharing in San Francisco that I broke off with Donald.

But, as for my son's business, we are still working at it.

Behind these scenes, over the years, I came to know my daughter Louee well and even better after she twigged me to the fact that an apartment was vacant in Albany, CA, next door to her own. This has been a wonderful arrangement, at least for me. I have come to admire and respect that lady and I always have loved her sweet, generous, loving and son Woody, who is dyslexic from oxygen deprivation at birth.

I have grown closer to my whole family: my Catholic son, Steffen, and his lovely and effective wife Kay, a knowledgeable Korean lady who teaches at the University of California part-time, while Steffen paints and wall-papers home interiors on his own.

I am crazy about their two kids, Jimmy Cheong-soo and Kathleen Ok-soo, who are lively, well-behaved and both very clever. Also, I have come to know, appreciate and love my two biggest grandchildren, Paul's son, Patrick, now 18 and entering the University of California at Davis in the Fall; and Jessica, nearing 15, who was graduated from Junior High and works at a florist shop, where her artistic ability can be utilized. Paul recently married his long-time sweetheart Nina Serrano, a poet, producer, writer and political activist. So far, they seem deliriously happy.(His marriage with Susie ended in divorce not too long after I returned to the U.S. in the early 70's.)

So here I am, approaching 73. I still have friends all over the world. I have a wonderful family. I have reasonably good health.

Hodee as a rabbit at an Organ Club event.
Oakland, CA. c. 1984

Other Books by H.W. Edwards

Anatomy of Revisionism, Stockholm 1979, Aurora Edition.

Labor Aristocracy, Mass Base of Social Democracy, Stockholm 1978, Aurora Edition.

Labor Aristocracy, Mass Base of Social Democracy, Second Edition, Vallejo, California, 2024, Estuary Press.